"I'm going in," he s

"What?" She watched aghast as Ethan flicked the latch on the horse's stall. Her hand went out to his arm. It was hard as a rock and she withdrew almost instantly, embarrassed.

Ethan took one step into the stall and Sage held her breath.

"Easy, boy," he said. The horse eyed him warily from the corner.

Her eyes couldn't help but trace the rugged lines of his biceps, their well-defined curves hinting at the raw strength of this man before her.

"I reckon we should start with some quiet talking," he said. "He's scared, and we need to be the ones to show him his fear isn't necessary."

Okay... Maybe this was a mistake. "This isn't some Hollywood movie, Ethan," she said, agitated by both his words and the way he was looking at her, like he was drawing her out of herself and everything that up to ten minutes ago had been quite comfortable, thank you very much.

Dear Reader,

Get your sunblock ready, and prep your taste buds for coffee and Vegemite—we're off to sunny Australia, where the snakes and spiders aren't the only things concerning our veterinary heroes! I had such fun with this one, bringing our wounded horse whisperer and his outback love interest to life. I hope you can soak up some sunshine through these pages.

Becky Wicks

xxx

TEMPTED BY THE OUTBACK VET

BECKY WICKS

Harlequin

MEDICAL ROMANCE

Harlequin®
MEDICAL ROMANCE

ISBN-13: 978-1-335-94259-3

Tempted by the Outback Vet

Harlequin Enterprises ULC
22 Adelaide St. West, 41st Floor
Toronto, Ontario M5H 4E3, Canada
www.Harlequin.com

Printed in U.S.A.

Recycling programs for this product may not exist in your area.

Born in the UK, **Becky Wicks** has suffered interminable wanderlust from an early age. She's lived and worked all over the world, from London to Dubai, Sydney, Bali, New York City and Amsterdam. She's written for the likes of *GQ*, *Hello!*, *Fabulous* and *Time Out*, and has written a host of YA romance, plus three travel memoirs—*Burqalicious*, *Balilicious* and *Latinalicious* (HarperCollins, Australia). Now she blends travel with romance for Harlequin and loves every minute! Find her on X @bex_wicks and subscribe at beckywicks.com.

Books by Becky Wicks

Harlequin Medical Romance

Enticed by Her Island Billionaire
Falling Again for the Animal Whisperer
Fling with the Children's Heart Doctor
White Christmas with Her Millionaire Doc
A Princess in Naples
The Vet's Escape to Paradise
Highland Fling with Her Best Friend
South African Escape to Heal Her
Finding Forever with the Single Dad
Melting the Surgeon's Heart
A Marriage Healed in Hawaii

Buenos Aires Docs

Daring to Fall for the Single Dad

Visit the Author Profile page
at Harlequin.com for more titles.

Dedicated to Paul and Campbell, two handsome
excuses to visit Australia for real.

CHAPTER ONE

SAGE STEPPED CLOSER to the paddock gate cautiously, the scraps bucket held tight in her hands. Storm was all action and nervous energy, rearing up and bucking violently at the sight of her.

'Steady, boy!' She flinched as the horse's hooves slammed to the sandy ground, his eyes wild with distress. This was the third week in a row that Storm had been inconsolable, refusing to let anyone near him. Ellie shuffled just behind her, twirling a strand of her sun-bleached blonde hair around one finger, as her young veterinary assistant often did when she was thinking.

'I just don't know what to do, Ells.' Sage's voice came out strained. 'I mean, look at him. I can't even get close enough to examine him! If anything he's getting worse. The mayor is going to want answers soon and, right now, I don't have any. Zero.'

Sage's heart ached. Feeling helpless never had sat well with her, especially where animals were involved—it brought back too many bad memories—and Abigail's husband, Amber Creek's beloved Mayor Jarrah Warragul, had brought Storm to her, convinced she could apply her years of veterinary expertise to help convert the wild animal into the doting pet his eleven-year-old wanted. Lucie, Sage's favourite of her best friend's three crazy kids, was beyond excited for rides through the outback on her very first horse, and at this rate Sage was going to have to let the whole family down, hard.

Ellie gave her shoulder a gentle squeeze, still quite understandably hesitant to step her petite frame much closer. 'Did you think any more about what the mayor said, about that vet we saw on TV last month? The one who calmed that uncontrollable racehorse?'

Sage nodded slowly as the image of the equine vet's face flashed back into her brain, throwing her off track for a moment. Rugged, handsome, built like a soldier in a sunhat…the kind of man who lived a life outdoors and could wrestle a croc with one arm. The mayor had suggested she call him; in fact, when she hadn't taken his advice, he had told her just today that he would go ahead and arrange things, which she hadn't told Ellie yet. It was more than humiliating, knowing she hadn't been good enough for the job.

'Ethan Matthews. Yes,' she said on a sigh. 'He used some kind of pressure-point massage to relax that horse.' She frowned as his features grew clearer in her mind's eye. The equine vet was bordering on being the sexiest man alive and not just because of the way his muscles rippled beneath his shirt like a sculpted masterpiece. He radiated the kind of magnetism that could stir something primal in a corpse, even through the TV screen. There should have been nothing more attractive to her than a guy who'd devoted his entire life to caring for animals, the same as she had, but this was her territory. She'd never had anyone else come in and take over before.

'Yes, him,' Ellie said with a dreamy sigh. 'I kind of wanted to *be* that horse.'

Ellie giggled into her hair and Sage rolled her eyes. The two of them had watched the vet in action intently for about ten minutes before realising they were both admiring a lot more than his horsemanship.

'He's supposed to be the best you can get when it comes to problematic horses. And Storm is definitely problematic. Look at poor Karma!' Ellie pointed out.

Sage looked at her newest gelding, Karma, who snorted obstinately from the corner of the paddock. He was doing better after his surgery, but she had her suspicions the healing horse just didn't want to provoke Storm in the same space.

Sage finally told Ellie that Ethan was flying in

tomorrow, and Ellie pretended she wasn't excited about it, even though her eyes practically bugged out of her head. Ethan lived in Queensland, and he was known for some pretty weird holistic practices, which felt more infuriating the more Sage thought about it. She'd been used to handling things her own way for the best part of six long years, and now they were just supposed to let some TV celebrity come in and take over?

'Maybe some of his methods might actually work?' Ellie suggested cautiously, eyeing Sage's fierce scowl.

Sage crossed to Karma, careful not to spook the wide-eyed Storm, who watched her every move suspiciously. 'Don't mind us, buddy,' Ellie told him, keeping close behind her.

She didn't have a choice about Ethan's so-called methods, she thought gloomily. Jarrah wanted him here, and, besides, the horse was too dangerous and unpredictable to have around his growing family. Abigail was five months pregnant with their fourth child and what if this unruly beast got a little too wild, a little too close to her? It didn't bear thinking about! Everyone here adored the mayor and his family, Sage most of all. She would be eternally grateful for the soft cushion they'd given her to land on six years ago when she'd driven into town, looking for work. Abigail knew everything about her past, too: the bushfire that had rendered her an orphaned child at ten years old, the fact that she might have prevented it if she hadn't been such a silly, disobedient kid, and that weird, sudden break-up with Bryce too, just weeks before she'd rocked up here.

Abigail had unbottled Sage years ago, along with the wine they had taken to sharing most Friday nights, and Sage was incredibly thankful that she'd been able to talk to someone about it all. It wasn't as though she went around telling just anyone *why* she'd grown up in the care of a foster family in Perth. Just the thought of all the animals that must have died that night when the fire had spread and killed her family, and Juni too—the best dog who'd ever lived—devastated her.

Keep on moving, keep busy, be a good vet, be good to your community, help the animals.

That was her strategy for life. It seemed to be working most of the time, except for when she saw a dog in distress. That always brought all the trauma rushing back, along with the overwhelming guilt.

Sage squinted against the sun. Why exactly was the thought of Ethan Matthews coming here unsettling her like this? He might well be an arrogant showbiz equine expert, but so what?

Maybe it was something about the look on his face when the camera had panned in, she thought. As if he was carrying some kind of close-held secret he only ever shared with his horses. Something that reminded her of herself.

* * *

The morning sun warmed her tense shoulders as Sage stood with her arms folded over the fence, chewing her lip distractedly under the wide-brimmed hat. She called out to Storm, who ignored her. He'd been restless all night again, snorting and pacing as if an invisible phantom were on his tail. It had taken even longer than usual to coerce him between the stall and the paddock with a broom handle.

The rumble of a truck caught her ears. Turning around, she felt her breath catch as the door of the red pickup swung open and then she was watching Ethan Matthews jump to the dusty ground. All six-foot-something of him.

The sunlight streamed across his broad shoulders, forcing her gaze to the contours of his biceps and the dark, almost jet-black thickness of his hair. He wore it scraped back into a rough, manly ponytail at the nape of his neck and he moved with a quiet confidence that made Sage's pulse quicken. She took him all in as he strode towards her in jeans. A forest-green T-shirt moulded to his sculpted torso, muscular thighs visible through every stretch of denim.

Holy hell...

'Dr Dawson?' He was in front of her, extending a big hand, fixing her with the most piercing blue eyes she'd ever seen. They were striking, rimmed with a deep green, and were more bewitching the longer she looked at them. She was suddenly aware they were roaming her face inquisitively, turning her cheeks into beetroots. 'Great to finally meet you.'

Finally? She bit back a grimace. So, he'd been anticipating showing up here for a while, then. Knowing the mayor as she did, he'd have waited at least two weeks out of the three before making the call. It wasn't as if he didn't trust her. He'd probably just realised she clearly didn't have the right experience for this task.

Sage adjusted her hat, willing her heart to calm down. She wanted to stay annoyed, but Ethan Matthews was so good-looking it was almost too much to take in—how were they not constantly doing close-ups of his eyes on TV? He was brooding from a distance, but this close the effect was devastating. Maybe they were afraid of hypnotising the nation. At any rate, nope. Such charm and charisma would *not* work on her.

'Dr Matthews, thanks for coming on such short notice,' she said after a rather awkward silence.

His grip was strong. That green shirt was doing strange things to her insides too; he either hit the gym every single day for an hour or so, or he'd honed his physique purely from wrestling wayward horses. Either way, he was likely all style over substance; he probably had a huge ego too, having everyone telling him how great he was all the time. Why was she feeling considerably hotter than she had been five minutes ago?

'Ethan, please,' he said, catching her eyes and holding them in a way that made her feel as though she'd forgotten to put on clothes this morning. This was nothing like when she'd first seen Bryce with his shaggy hair and oversized backpack, she thought, agitated all over again.

Wait…why was she comparing Ethan to Bryce?

'Ethan. I appreciate you being here. It's a long way from Queensland,' she said, forcing herself to be polite.

'I go where I'm needed,' he replied with a trace of a smirk. 'I'm sure I can help the mayor get this horse into shape in no time.'

'Well, good luck with that,' she said, more snippily than she intended. Oh, to be that confident and self-assured! 'Three weeks in and I've barely been able to meet his eyes. The only way I can get him to move anywhere is by waving the broom at him. I feel like an evil witch.'

At that, Ethan stifled a laugh, which annoyingly, rather pleased her to hear. Then his eyes trailed the whole length of her body from her boots right up to her face. Sage had never felt so exposed in her life. Even more than before, she certainly did not want this cocky man all up in her business for longer than he had to be. But still, the way he was looking at her made her swallow hard…

'I'll take you to Storm,' she said, flustered.

CHAPTER TWO

IN THE PADDOCK, Sage watched Ethan's eyes lock onto Storm with sharp focus. Keeping his movements slow and steady, he followed her to the stall of their troubled animal patient, ignoring the creature's indignant snorts and holding up both his hands. Sage stood at his side, casting secret glances his way, taking in the decisive slope of his nose, the sharp angle of his cheekbones. What would it feel like to have those big man hands on her own skin? His forearms were so thick with muscle, she half expected to see him pick up Storm with one arm...

'I'm going in,' he said.

'What?'

She watched aghast as Ethan flicked the latch on the stall door, causing the horse to stop in his tracks and stare straight at him.

'What are you doing?' Panic coiled in her belly as her hand went out to his arm. It was hard as a rock and she withdrew it almost instantly, embarrassed. But he didn't even have the broomstick to move him with, or to use as defence.

'I wouldn't go in there. I just told you, he hasn't let anyone close…' she started. Was this really the right approach, so soon? But Ethan didn't appear to be listening to her. He took one step into the stall and Sage held her breath, waiting for the horse to bolt, or, worse, lunge for them both.

'Easy, boy,' he said, almost under his breath. The horse eyed him warily from the corner. Ethan started lowering himself at a snail's pace to his haunches, murmuring gentle words of reassurance. Storm was still looking at him suspiciously down the length of his long nose, and Sage's heart was banging like a drum. What was he doing? Surely, this tactic would not end well! Still, whatever he was doing, her eyes couldn't help but trace the rugged lines of his biceps, their well-defined curves hinting at the raw strength of this man before her.

'I reckon we should start with some quiet talking,' he said. 'He's scared, and we need to be the ones to show him his fear isn't necessary.'

Sage almost snorted despite herself. 'Quiet talking?' She had already tried that, as well as begging the horse fervently with her dignity firmly squashed beneath her own muddy boots, all to no avail.

Ethan nodded, eyes still fixed on Storm. 'Horses

understand everything about our tone and intentions. We have to speak to his spirit first.'

OK...maybe this was a mistake.

'This isn't some Hollywood movie, Ethan. It's not that simple,' she heard herself say, agitated by both his words and the way he was looking at her, as if he was drawing her out of herself and everything that up to ten minutes ago had been quite comfortable, thank you very much.

Ethan gave a short laugh. 'Trust me, he's waiting for someone to understand him.'

Sage just looked at him. What was she supposed to do with this? She hadn't actually heard much of what Ethan had said to that horse on TV; the focus had been on his actions, his strong, confident energy. He had all the right qualifications, a background in veterinary care that stretched back more than a decade; he'd even been on an episode of *Vets in the Wild*, where he'd tamed a stallion that had already stomped a man down and left him fighting for his life in hospital, but this was just...well—not quite what she'd expected. This was supposed to have been her issue to handle, her problem to solve, yet she was more confused now than she'd been before.

She bit her tongue as he held out a hand slowly, cautiously. Surely it was only a matter of seconds before he regretted this too; Storm was wilder than she could handle with her experience alone and, she'd assumed, Ethan's too, despite being the star of the nation. To her shock, though, the horse took a tentative step towards him.

'He's listening to you, he's responding,' she said in awe, covering her mouth with her hand. OK, so maybe he wasn't just all mouth and muscles as she'd assumed. She'd gone as far as assuming the camera had lied, or they'd at least done some clever editing. But here he was. In the flesh. Succeeding where she'd failed. So infuriating.

Ethan continued to murmur soft words of encouragement from his lowered position on the ground and soon the horse was sniffing warily at his outstretched hand. Sage watched, afraid to move for what felt like at least an hour but was probably only three minutes.

'So, are you a wizard or something?' she asked him eventually, feeling silly instantly.

Ethan finally tore his gaze away long enough to chuckle at her under his breath. No sooner had he flashed her a half-smile, however, than Storm was scrambling backwards and rearing up on his hind legs, spooked by something all over again.

'Move!' Ethan's reflexes were as fast as the horse's. He rose to full standing and before she had a chance to react he was throwing himself between her and the snorting, wild-eyed animal. Sage gasped for breath as Ethan yanked her against him, holding out his other hand to Storm as they backed away slowly through the stall door.

'Steady,' he implored quietly. Did he mean her, or the horse?

Her whole body tensed with shock as he shielded her from the threat of Storm's powerful hooves and she didn't know whether to be impressed by his quick reaction or annoyed with her own slow one as he latched the door behind them. Storm hoofed at the floor repeatedly, kicking up the dirt. Sage's back was still pressed hard against Ethan's chest, his flexed arm like a giant safety belt across her abdomen. For a moment she couldn't even move. Then, embarrassed and maybe more than a little undermined by this man who was still a stranger on her turf, she uncoiled herself.

'I told you, he hasn't let anyone close, so *why* did you do that?'

Ethan fixed his blue gaze onto hers. 'And I told you, Dr Dawson, he's waiting for someone to understand him. He'll only know that we do if we back off now.'

His tone was gruff and assertive and somehow managed to both irritate her and turn her on at the same time. She smoothed down her overalls and was about to tell him that maybe this hadn't been the mayor's best idea when he cut her off by extending a hand, straight at her face. She blinked as he swiped something from the rim of her hat, and a wisp of straw floated to the ground.

'This will take a while. But I'll take the case,'

he said. 'No broom necessary.' Then he tilted his head at her in a brief, courteous bow before turning and leaving the stable. Sage followed him out into the sunlight, squinting, heart still racing. Ethan didn't bother opening the gate to the paddock. He simply scaled the five metal bars with one jump like a two-legged show pony in jeans. Then he swung it wide open just for her to walk through after him.

Sage bit down on the inside of her cheek. How dare he just stroll in and make everything look so easy? OK, so this man had made more progress with Storm in a matter of minutes than she'd made in three whole weeks, but the magic show had to end at some point. Storm was unpredictable at best. He could take many weeks, even months of training. Ethan's confidence would likely wear off just as hers had, but she still might be stuck with him for ages until that happened!

Why was she suddenly wondering how close he'd be sleeping to her? Of course, he'd stay at Yukka Guest House, just like everyone else!

Leading Ethan into the clinic, Sage was acutely aware of his tall, muscular frame behind her. She glanced back at him as he looked around, taking in the examination rooms and medical equipment, the poster of the horse with the kookaburra on its head that hung over the reception desk, and the row of slightly dusty cactus plants in the window. He exuded an aura of quiet intensity that charged the room.

'Nice place. How long have you been here, Dr Dawson?' He ran a finger over one of the cacti as if daring it to prick him.

'Call me Sage. And it's coming up for six years now,' she told him, just as Ellie appeared from the back with an owner and her rabbit, its leg freshly bandaged from its brush with a snare. She introduced them and watched Ellie and the rabbit's female twenty-something owner flush. Both women actually fluttered their eyelashes! Ethan fielded questions from them with brief replies, while casting his gaze first to her, then back to them, causing her to roll her eyes, as well as smooth her frizzy hair from her face so many times it went static.

Ruffled, she called Yukka Guest House in Amber Creek to ask about a room, warning her eyeballs to stop roving over his face from across the reception. But she couldn't help it; he was probably one of the most striking men she'd ever laid eyes on. Not that a TV star with an ego the size of the moon would look twice at someone like her, covered in dust and straw on the outside…a bit of a mess on the inside most days, too.

She tutted to herself. That wasn't entirely fair; she wasn't ugly. And she wasn't always covered in dust and straw either. It was just that she was…well…what man would want to deal with all her baggage? The orphaned child, fostered by a wealthy miner, given all the privileges and advantages she could've dreamed of: a caring new family who weren't her own, but who loved her anyway, an education at one of Australia's most prestigious veterinary institutions, money, freedom...yet who still couldn't date a guy without the same profound sense of hopelessness swallowing her senses, reducing her to an undatable weirdo, incapable of forging an emotional connection. She hadn't slept with more than three people since that doomed relationship with Bryce, six whole years ago. She probably had cobwebs. Not that those three men hadn't all tried to pursue her afterwards; she just had a habit of keeping her heart locked up where it couldn't be broken any more. They all got tired of her emotionally stunted self eventually.

'I've booked you my regular room at Yukka Guest House for tonight,' she told him when they were alone again, as an image of him lounging in bed forced her eyes back away from him. 'After that you can decide if you want to stay there or move...'

He quirked an eyebrow. 'Your regular room?'

'The room I reserve for locums and visitors,' she corrected herself. Could he read her mind or something? He laughed softly. The sound of it made her skin prickle and she cleared her throat.

'That was pretty remarkable, back there,' she

said before she could stop herself. 'I've never seen anyone calm any horse so quickly. Even if it didn't last.'

Ethan gave a modest shrug. 'Just takes patience. And reading their body language.'

The way he said 'body language' while looking at her...

Oh, my.

Sage started quickly tidying up some scattered papers on the front desk. In her hurry, a sheet fell to the floor and it floated in the draught against his leather boot. He bent to retrieve it just as she did, and their hands brushed over the piece of paper. Sage sucked in a sharp breath. On reflection, it was so loud she could've sworn Ellie heard it in the exam room. It must have spoken volumes about the way he was tangling up her insides already in this confined space, but if Ethan noticed, he said nothing.

'So, Mr Famous,' she said bluntly, shoving the papers back onto a pile on the desk and finally retrieving Storm's file. 'I've seen you on TV. How long have you had this gift with horses?'

'Gift?' He smirked, placing the file under his arm as he made a thing of eyeing her exam certificates, framed in a row on the wall. Bachelor of Veterinary Science, Member of the Australian Veterinary Association, and also a specialised postgraduate qualification highlighting her advanced training in veterinary surgical procedures.

'You seem to have some kind of qualification that I don't,' she said pointedly. 'I don't even think you can study for what you can do. Therefore it's a gift, isn't it?' Sage hoped the comment didn't inflate his ego any further. But she'd said it now. His eyes met hers, and her pulse quickened. He was so intense. She'd just caught his bergamot-like scent too: citrus and wildflowers and horses and man. The smell stirred something in her, made her heart start to beat even faster. Maybe she was just a little starstruck, she reasoned, because of the whole TV thing. How irritating.

Ethan rubbed his neck self-consciously. 'I wouldn't call it a gift. Just skills I've picked up over the years. Helps that I'm as stubborn as most horses,' he said wryly.

Sage sensed his humility was genuine and felt a momentary stab of guilt at her prickliness. 'Still, your techniques are quite different from how we practise around here,' she followed.

'I hope that won't be a problem.'

For a moment, she glimpsed a flicker of rebellion in his eyes and she fought the instinctive desire to tell him there was a way of doing things around here—*her* way. Her way hadn't worked so far, had it? Not with Storm. And the *mayor* wanted him here.

'We open at seven a.m.,' she said instead, motioning for the door. She walked him across the dusty forecourt to his vehicle, simultaneously flustered and intrigued. 'I understand you'll want more time with Storm tomorrow...'

'And the other horses,' he said, opening the car door and leaning on it, eyeing her over his crossed arms. 'I need to see how he interacts with the others. I'll be here early, if that's OK.'

She fished around in the giant pocket of her overalls, then handed him a key. 'Sure, that's the key to the back. You'll find the coffee machine there. If it doesn't start, just give it a firm kick.'

'I'll be sure to do that.'

'Any problems, I live just over there.' She pointed to her humble cabin beyond the tree line, where she'd been shacked up since arriving. It was modest to say the least, but it had become somewhat of a home while she tended the small native plant garden around it and kept the wildlife from moving in. Better than paying rent in town.

'You live here too?' he asked, seemingly surprised.

'Yeah, I'm still trying to figure out the irrigation system so we can grow more than cacti but...'

'Can I see?'

She watched as Ethan closed the car door again and made for her cabin. Following him, she prayed she hadn't left any undies out to dry. Thankfully she hadn't, but he seemed curious about her rock garden, and the compost pile she'd constructed to recycle organic waste. Before she knew it, they were discussing the plans for the drip irrigation system, which would eventually deliver water directly to the base of plants, minimising evaporation. He told her he lived on a homestead with his dad that included an equine centre for troubled horses and prime grazing that she knew they only had in Queensland. His late mother had been adamant they turn it into the most climate-conscious place they could for the whole community to enjoy, before she died.

'I'm so sorry you lost your mother,' she told him as the awkwardness snaked around her like a living thing. How could her own mum's smiling face not come back to her, the second he shared that information? Ethan simply nodded at the ground, ending the conversation by making for his ute again.

Suddenly Sage was wondering if he had a wife, or a girlfriend, waiting at this homestead, and found herself looking at his left hand. No ring. That didn't mean anything though, really. And why should she care? Still, they stood there at the vehicle for just a second too long for it to be comfortable. And as his ute rumbled away, she felt the strangest sensation that her entire world had just shifted completely on its axis.

CHAPTER THREE

ETHAN SCANNED THE horizon over his coffee mug. The landscape beyond the borders of the clinic seemed endless, hugged by jagged dunes and rugged, red-earthed wilderness. It was beautiful around here, even at six-thirty a.m., and remote. It wasn't as if he didn't know remote, though.

He and his dad lived this way themselves for the most part in Queensland, just them and the horses and dogs, away from the noise and traffic and...memories, but this was something else. The nearest town, Amber Creek, was four miles away. Babs, the funny and kind woman at the guest house, hadn't been able to stop staring at him when he'd first arrived; was he that much of a celebrity here? The thought was grating.

He could tell Sage wasn't particularly keen to have him here either. He would get her on board, show her it wasn't all camera magic and celebrity draw that kept people calling him where other vets failed, but still he probably shouldn't have agreed to all the TV stuff in the first place. It was

just that they'd offered him a lot of money. And
with everything he and Dad had wanted to do
with the land to honour Mum's dream, their plans
for the self-sufficiency workshops, the rainwater-
harvesting system and solar panels she'd started
implementing before the cancer stole her mobil-
ity and mind—well, they'd needed a significant
injection of funds. But there was still so much to
do. And the mayor of Amber Creek had offered
him a significant amount of money to treat Storm.
Almost as much as the network.

Clutching his coffee, he rested a boot on the
gate of the paddock and sipped the scorching
black brew. Dr Dawson… Sage, had been right.
He'd had to kick the machine pretty hard to get a
decent cup of coffee out of it. He'd also relocated
a redback spider more than once over the last few
days. Little guy had made a home for himself,
nestled amongst the filters.

'I'm almost done, Ethan!' The stable hand,
Billy, had shown up ten minutes after him. The
lanky kid, dressed in denim shorts and a baseball
hat, was mucking out the stalls now, neatly avoiding Storm. Ethan raised his cup at him, ready to
address the situation when the kid was out of the
way. The horse was snorting again, not as angrily
as he had done on day one, but Storm's sweat-
soaked coat was reflecting the morning sunlight
in a way that concerned him. This was one un-

settled animal. The problem was, he didn't know why yet.

He was just placing his chipped mug back by the kickable coffee machine in the back room, wondering yet again why there was a giant NO NAKED FLAMES IN THE KITCHEN PLEASE! sign on the wall, when a shadow appeared behind him in the doorway.

'Morning, Ethan.'

The light cast a warm golden glow over Sage's wavy chestnut hair, loose again today, falling around her shoulders from the same wide-brimmed hat. For a moment he just stood there, and she stood opposite, smiling from one corner of her pretty mouth, seemingly taking in his clean checked shirt and jeans, and the brown leather boots he'd stormed across a thousand paddocks in.

'I like the boots,' Sage quipped.

'Thanks. They were a gift,' he said. Sage nodded from the doorway as if waiting for him to tell a story. Of course, he wouldn't. Carrie had bought him these boots eight years ago, right after they declared themselves an item. If only he'd known back then that the footwear would last longer than their relationship; that she'd wind up with his best friend while he was blinded to it all by grief, reeling from losing Mum.

Sage blinked, offering a slightly nervous laugh before skirting around him. 'I just need a...'

'Right, a coffee.' He moved quickly, but not before catching the scent of her: freshly showered, maybe a splash of fragrance, something floral. She went about putting a new mug under the ancient contraption and hit the button under 'flat white'. Then she pulled her phone out, scanned it unseeingly and slid it straight back into her pocket while his eyes fixated on her movements.

So, here it was again. The same unsettling attraction to her that he hadn't known exactly what to do with on day one. It had probably made things a little awkward, all the little silences between their exchanges. Sage Dawson kind of reminded him of Carrie. And that wasn't exactly a good thing. They were the same slight build, the same height, five-foot-five-ish, with eyes that unpicked you. There was something about her intelligence and determination that had caught him off guard and put him in his place, and she never seemed starstruck like the woman at the guest house. Having her remind him of Carrie wasn't ideal. His ex-fiancé was probably just waking up to another Brisbane sunrise in the fancy penthouse apartment she and Cam had bought after their wedding: traitors, both of them.

'So, how's Storm this morning? Did you get a chance to examine him yet?' Sage was still staring at the empty coffee cup, and the silent machine.

'I was waiting for Billy to finish mucking out. We don't want to startle him.'

'Oh, so Billy showed up.' Sage frowned and raised a knee at the machine. He grinned as she gave it a hearty kick from below, sending the mug flying. Deftly he caught it mid-flight and handed it back, and she pulled a face behind her hair as their fingers brushed. There. Again. She'd started out all spiky but after they'd talked in her garden the other day, he was almost sure he'd detected a spark of something else. That *spark* was something he hoped he'd been imagining. The last thing he needed was another woman looking at him all googly-eyed because of how the network portrayed him—they'd cut out most of his words and focused instead on long shots of his body and close-ups of his muscles as if he was nothing more than a gym rat—which he was, to some degree, he supposed. Keeping strong was imperative, plus it kept his mind from going into dark corners it would do best not to revisit.

But there was something different about Sage, too. As if she was looking beyond all that. As if she had the capacity to reach places he'd barriered shut for a reason. Good thing he wouldn't be here long; he'd fix up this horse and be out of here in no time. Back to his father, who needed him.

Sage took her coffee outside, and this time he didn't leap over the fence as he had a few times now. Force of habit. It was just what he did back home. She seemed as conflicted as Billy when he walked towards Storm's stall. They both stood behind him as he flicked the latch again, but soon they disappeared somewhere into the silence on the periphery, as people usually did when it came to the horses.

He'd always been this way, so deeply connected to the animals in a way most others couldn't understand. Except Dad, who'd done it all his life, too. This horse had been growing increasingly restless. He heard Billy whisper as much to Sage, but Ethan hoped his presence would offer some kind of solace to the creature. As it had the first time, right before Storm had reared up and almost taken their eyes out.

'Easy, boy,' he said, holding out a steady hand so the horse could see he meant no harm. Slowly he approached Storm, and noticed the animal's ears flicking back and forth, his nostrils flaring with every breath.

'What made you this way, boy? Or who?' he murmured softly, stepping closer. He allowed Storm to sniff his palm before gently stroking the horse's velvety muzzle. Sage held her breath behind him, but this time he didn't break his focus. That was what had happened before, he realised. It had kept him awake for a good hour extra that first night. For the first time in a long time while dealing with a distressed horse he had looked away, distracted. By Sage. She'd asked if he was a wizard.

There *was* something about her that unsettled

him, more than just her likeness to Carrie. He'd seen it increasingly these past few days, watching her going about her business, a faraway look in her eyes. They had as much pain locked behind them as this horse sometimes. Like looking in a mirror, he thought, not looking away from Storm. He was still stroking his snout—this was some form of success at least. To his relief, Storm's eyes softened further at the touch, and he let out a quiet nicker as if to say thank you.

'I can tell he trusts you. At least he's starting to, mate,' Billy said behind him. Sage immediately asked him to be quiet.

It wouldn't be smart to push things, he thought. This was enough for now. 'The exam can wait,' he told them, backing out of the stall again. Billy left to answer a call. Sage watched intently as Ethan reached an arm over the railing and gave Storm another soft stroke, along his chestnut neck this time.

'How do you…?' Her voice, before she cut her question short, was tinged with a kind of begrudging respect that tickled him.

'I don't know, Sage, you tell me,' he said, biting back a smile. He led her back outside. It was getting warm already and he removed his hat to tighten his hair in the band at the back of his sticky neck. He didn't miss Sage's eyes trailing down the front of his shirt, all the way to his belt, where they hovered for just a moment too long.

'My dad, his father, and his before that,' he said, by way of further explanation as her gaze flicked back up to his. He locked his eyes to hers as he adjusted his belt. He didn't need to. It just felt tighter after having her look at it. 'They're communicating with us in their own way. We just have to tune in to what they're saying, like finding the right frequency on a radio. They harbour fear and pain just like we do. And they can be blissfully peaceful. So calm and tranquil. Which humans are not, generally speaking.'

'You're intuitively understanding their pain from the signals they transmit.'

'Kind of.'

Sage studied his face again thoughtfully, waving a fly away from her face, then fanning her white shirt, which was open just enough at the neck to reveal sun-tanned skin and freckles. There was a flicker of hurt in her voice now, a hint at whatever pain she harboured herself deep below the surface. 'Well,' she said quickly. 'Whatever it is you're doing, it's working.'

Ethan watched her run a brief exam on Karma. There were five horses here, considerably less than his herd of twenty-plus, give or take, depending on the equine patients who stayed for variable lengths of time. Billy had explained this morning how three of them were his, including Karma. He worked in the stable and grounds here to subsidise their upkeep. Sage was the chief vet and, as far as he could see, she had a limited staff on the rota. Ellie and…that was it. It seemed like a lot of work for a skeleton crew but he wasn't about to question or judge.

He had got the impression, that first day in her garden, that she had poured all her efforts into this place because it was more than just a job to her. This was her entire life. No wonder she hadn't wanted some strange vet waltzing into what she'd built and upending it all. He also got the feeling that this was her whole life for another reason too. He knew better than to push, though. There was the matter of his own internal scars; he'd hate to be forced to discuss all those. Losing Mum to cancer three months after her diagnosis was one thing…two years on and Dad was only just starting to come out the other side. Then there was the ultimate gut-punch on top, knowing his best friend and his ex-fiancée were probably happier than they'd ever been now that Ethan's own grief and his horses were no longer in the equation, living their city dream in wedded bliss.

He could still hear Cam's words to Carrie. It was far too easy to picture himself standing right outside the door of that hotel suite all over again, the blood from the cat he'd just done emergency surgery on still fresh on his shirt.

'How can you stand Ethan when he does all that weird horsey stuff? You know he'll never

love you as much as his animals, right, Carrie?
You won't ever come first for him.'

    'Don't be so mean. His mum just died!'

    'Is that why you don't want to tell him about
us yet?'

Catching himself, he snatched up a bridle from
the hook on the wall and threw it to her. 'Tack
him up,' he said. Thirteen months and three
weeks since the day he'd found out about their
affair, and it still had the power to stab him in the
gut, as if it had happened only yesterday.

    'Now?'

    'He's healing just fine.'

Sage stared at him, incredulous. 'I don't ride
Karma. He's Billy's horse. And are you sure he's
ready? He's not long been castrated.'

    'He's fine,' he said. 'It'll probably be good for
Storm to see you riding him, too. Show him what
his role's supposed to be. You said the mayor
bought him for his daughter, over the phone?'

Sage shook her head at her feet a moment, and
he realised that despite her growing tolerance to
his presence, and their undeniable attraction,
she still harboured a little scepticism over his
so-called unconventional methods. It wasn't as
though he was the only qualified veterinarian in
the world who knew horses and their minds, but
for people like Sage, who'd gone down a more
traditional path with all her certificates from top
establishments…well, sometimes they needed

convincing. Not that he had the time for all that. If people didn't trust his 'weird horsey stuff', that was their problem. The results spoke for themselves. Karma was clearly well and could do with a ride after his time off.

A call came from beyond the fence. Ellie, Sage's veterinary assistant, was waving a phone at them. 'Sage, it's Lance, down at Redgum Ridge. A kookaburra just crashed into his glass door, and it's in pretty bad shape. He doesn't want to move it.'

'Lance's place is beyond the bridge, the one that's closed,' Sage explained to Ethan, chewing her lip. 'I can't get the ute through.' She cast speculative eyes at him. Before he could even suggest it, Sage was striding back over to Billy.

'Do you mind if I take Karma out?' she asked him, pressing a gentle hand to Karma's silky forelock.

'Not at all. I think he's ready, too.'

'Great. I'll have to take more supplies than I can carry. We're going to need a cage to bring it back.' Then she looked at Ethan again, her gaze filled with the question.

'I'll go with you,' he replied. 'Billy, can you saddle up one more while I grab my bag?'

CHAPTER FOUR

'DR DAWSON?' LANCE, an older guy, maybe late fifties, stood in the doorway of the old run-down house, clutching their injured kookaburra protectively in his hands. 'I was watching TV. Then I heard the crash at the back door,' he explained. 'I thought someone was trying to break in, but when I went to check I found this poor fella just lying there all…wonky.'

'No worries, Lance, you did the right thing, calling us,' Sage said. 'This is Ethan Matthews, by the way. He's working with me for a while over at the clinic.'

Ethan stuck his hand out, noting the dishevelled hair, the crumpled shirt and the beer cans littering the porch. His own dad had gone this way for a while, after Mum died. Luckily Ethan and his sister had pulled him out of it. Jacqueline had been a total rock through the whole thing, though she'd suffered the loss in her own way. She always said she had to be strong for her husband, Mack, and she'd had the kids to think about when their mum had passed, too. He'd always maintained it was better to experience the full spectrum of emotions that orbited grief. Then Carrie had done what she'd done, and he'd blocked the whole damn lot of it out.

'You rode all the way out here,' Lance said, nodding towards the horses tied up out by bushes in the shade.

'The bridge is still out of action, remember?' she said kindly as he directed them inside. Lance furrowed his brow, as though he had actually forgotten.

'He doesn't leave this place much,' Sage whispered to Ethan in explanation as they followed the man inside. 'Not since he lost his wife.'

Ethan nodded. So he'd been right. Poor man.

Despite its old tin roof and weathered exterior, the house seemed quite cosy and well maintained on the inside. A cat unfurled itself lazily from the sofa and crept around Lance's legs as Sage instructed him to place the bird carefully on the small round table in the kitchen.

Together, they examined the kookaburra, gently probing it for signs of injury. Sage inspected its wings and feathers, murmuring softly to it under her breath as she did so. As they worked side by side, her green eyes seemed to glow even more with determination. Her loose chestnut hair fell in soft waves around her face, framing her delicate features. When she wasn't wearing the hat, she looked younger for some reason. She couldn't have been much younger than him though, and he was thirty-five. So much like Carrie, he thought again…only, the more he looked at Sage, the more he could see how different they really were.

Sage had a look that was entirely her own. Besides, being a city girl, Carrie wouldn't be seen dead in overalls. Looking back, she probably never would have ended up moving from Brisbane to the homestead as they'd planned to after they married. It was far too rustic out there, with way too many snakes and spiders for her to feel completely comfortable. Besides, she wasn't all *that* into horses really. They'd been an odd match from the start. She was an actress, fresh from Sydney. He'd met her the same night as Cam in the pub next to the theatre. The three of them had chatted for four solid hours, till Cam had murmured that he felt like a third wheel and left them to it.

Carrie used to love how he and his family had turned the old family cattle station into a successful equine centre and homestead, with plans for an eco-conscious community that would eventually, with all of their help, thrive around it. Mum had always dreamed of off-grid living, creating a hub for sustainable ventures and permaculture initiatives. Carrie had seemed so into it at first, talking about 'learning the bees', as his sister, Jacqueline, had done. His sister's honey was still the best for miles around, and she still came over every Saturday with Mack and his niece and nephew, who buzzed about the place more than the bees.

Carrie had helped Mum and Jacqueline with the bees a lot for the first couple of years, or just read her books and studied her lines in the hammock while he worked with the horses. She'd seemed happy, and it had shaken his world up when Dad had taken him aside one day and asked if everything was OK between them.

Dad had noticed Carrie was spending more time on her phone than she was engaging with them; more time out and about in the city with her friends than honouring plans she'd made to do things with *him*. She'd missed three farmers' markets in a row.

He'd thought if he proposed, things would get better. She'd always said they could wait for marriage—who knew when her latest show would go on tour? He'd agreed; after all, he'd been so busy being a vet, and working out in the fields with Dad and the horses. There had been plenty of time to plan a wedding, really, but he'd figured they would be doing it eventually so he'd asked her anyway.

For a while, things had got better; Carrie had got excited trying on dresses, sending him photos of vineyards and beaches and wine glasses and platters of cheese. Then Mum had died. And afterwards, when neither of them could agree on a date for the wedding—probably because she'd already started seeing Cam—she'd stopped coming to the homestead at all, saying he spent *too* much time with the horses, and that she found it all increasingly boring being with someone who didn't seem to enjoy the same things any more. Maybe she was right. But after several years together, she should have gone to him with all this. Instead she'd gone to Cam.

'Looks like a broken wing,' Sage was saying now, carefully holding the bird still.

'But there must be some internal damage too,' he mused. 'He's not moving much. We can take him back with us for further tests.'

Their hands touched briefly as he helped apply a splint and Sage seemed to be looking at him with a strange look on her face as he wrapped a towel gently around the bird, motioning for her to open the cage they'd brought with them.

'What?' he asked.

'You're good with the animals,' she said, and he frowned.

'Did you think I wouldn't be?'

'I don't know…you never know if what you see on TV is real or not any more,' she answered as he took over settling the kookaburra inside the cage on another fresh towel. 'And I'm not used to having a qualified partner for things like this.'

'Well, I'm here. And I'm totally real.'

'I see that now.'

The vulnerability in her eyes caught him off guard, and he found himself wondering if she'd had any partners at all lately, all the way out here.

'We should get this little guy back to the clinic, make sure he's OK,' she said, breaking whatever moment that had just been.

As they were leaving, Ethan got a glimpse of the bedroom through the hallway. Two broken windows. Peeling paint everywhere. He made a mental note to talk to Billy later about them possibly helping out with some repair work. It wouldn't take long to fix a few new glass panes and run a brush around. Unless that wasn't his place, he thought as he lifted the cage out carefully to the horses, telling Sage he'd carry it back. He'd only been here five minutes—of course it wasn't his place! He just wasn't the kind of guy who could stand around knowing someone might need help, as his dad had needed help; not when he could be doing something about it.

The vast outback surrounded them on all sides as he rode with the cage in front of him against the saddle. The silence seemed charged. 'Is he OK?' Sage asked stiffly.

'He's doing fine,' he replied, hoping it was true. The sun beat down on his back and the horses plodded along steadily, their hooves creating a comforting rhythm that was broken only by the occasional soft whinny. Ethan couldn't help but

marvel at the beauty of this wilderness: the rolling hills, the majestic gum trees reaching for
the sky. It wasn't home. He could never leave
Queensland permanently—his dad relied on him,
and his mum's living legacy was still under con-
struction—but despite its ferocious heat and un-
forgiving terrain, there was something inherently
peaceful about it.

Then Sage spoke.

'Does your wife or girlfriend mind all the travelling you do?'

Ethan hesitated, caught off guard by her personal question. How much did he need to reveal?

'Or your husband, or boyfriend, perhaps?' she
added with a rare smile.

He bit back a laugh. 'I don't do relationships
at all,' he said, keeping his tone light. Neither
of them mentioned the kangaroo that bounded
away into the distance from behind a bush as
they passed.

'Ah, I see,' she replied softly, her gaze focused
on the path ahead. Was that a small smirk on her
face? Did that sound like a 'typical bloke' thing
to say? It wasn't as if he could blurt out why he
didn't do relationships, and probably never would
again. 'I'm single. And I like it that way…for
now.'

He'd only added 'for now' so he wouldn't sound
too miserable. That wasn't how he felt most of the
time; in fact, he was starting to see a little light

through the fog of confusion and anger that had seen him confiding only in his horses, and pouring his grief into working out in his makeshift home gym for the last year. But he'd never get over it completely—who would? His best friend and his fiancée…such a cliche.

'So, what brought you to Amber Creek?' he asked her, realising an awkward silence had descended again.

Sage blew air through her nose and kept her eyes on the horizon. She told him how she'd floated around a lot before landing on this place, working with aboriginal tribes, and cultural and conservation programmes across various indigenous protected areas. She'd even worked at a koala reserve for a while. 'Guess I didn't know where I wanted to be, till I found this place.'

'Why's that?' he pressed, picturing how cute she'd look with several koalas clinging to her.

She told him about her friend, Abigail, the mayor's wife. How she'd helped her a lot. How she'd found it nice to be able to talk to someone about anything and everything. He told her how he used to have a friend like that. Ethan couldn't read the look on her face, but Sage was starting to drift somewhere in her mind again.

'How did she help you?'

'I guess I grew up pretty reserved after…well, after losing my parents. I mostly talked to the animals about it all, you know, like a weirdo.'

He flinched. Being a weirdo who talked to the animals. He knew all about that, too, but all he said was, 'I've met bigger weirdos, trust me.' They had the horses walking slowly, so as not to disturb the kookaburra, but he could feel his shirt starting to stick to his back. This Abigail had probably heard more about Sage's life than she'd ever share with him and it wasn't his job to pry.

'I'm so sorry you lost both your parents,' he couldn't help saying, picturing his mum again, how she'd used to wear a silly hat around the homestead, as Sage did around the clinic grounds. 'How old were you?'

That was OK to ask, right?

'I was ten when they both died,' she replied curtly, pulling Karma to a stop and leaping off. 'Anyway. It's all ancient history, right? Here we are.'

Ancient history? She'd lost *both* her parents at the same time?

Ethan hadn't even realised till now that they were back at the clinic already, and she was un-latching the front gate, sending a dust cloud up around her that swallowed her boots. She reached up for the cage, blowing her hair from her sticky face.

'I'll carry it from here. Can you take the horses back to Billy?' She squinted up at him. Her tone had turned strictly professional again now, with no room or time for personal stories.

'Yes, ma'am. I'll examine Storm now.'

'If he lets you,' she said drily.

Ethan opened his mouth to reply that he was sure Storm would, but decided against it. If she was so determined to be surprised every time he was good with an animal, let her be surprised when Storm let him in.

Ethan watched her walk purposefully up the path, where Ellie met her on the front steps. She stopped, then gave a quick glance back at him over her shoulder, and even from a distance he could see the apprehension in her body language. Sage already felt as though she'd told him too much about herself, but if it really was ancient history, why didn't it explain the lingering sadness he could feel ebbing out of her? What else had she endured? Now he needed to know more.

CHAPTER FIVE

SAGE WATCHED AS Ethan's fingers drummed rhyth-
mically on the wooden fence, his blue eyes narrowed in concentration. He had those damned
boots on again. He looked so hot in them. Last
night she'd dreamed about them—weren't they on
her kitchen floor, along with that denim shirt he
was wearing the other day? The details were kind
of blurry. In fact, the blurry and not so blurry
dreams about Ethan Matthews were getting out
of hand now, the more he seemed to crawl inside
her skull.

They had retreated to the shade of a nearby
tree, allowing Storm some space after his first
semi-exam. It was a semi-exam because Ethan
had so far managed only to lift one front leg.
Three days ago, after rescuing the kookaburra
together, which thankfully was now doing a lot
better, Ethan had tried to examine the unruly animal and failed. He'd spent an hour on the phone
to someone afterwards and later she'd found out
it was his father. He seemed to speak with him

every day, actually, and she envied that a little. Obviously they were close after losing his mother; they lived together at the homestead. What she wouldn't give to be able to pick up the phone to her biological dad—not that Ken wasn't there for her when she needed him. Her foster dad was amazing.

Even after showing some semblance of normality and trust towards Ethan in the stall, when it came to an exam, Storm just wasn't having it. Almost as if the horse didn't *want* anyone to see inside his head. 'Doesn't it bother you that he's still being so…hostile?' she said now, surprised at herself for actually being concerned that Ethan's methods weren't working—wasn't that what she'd expected, before he showed up? Ethan huffed a laugh, still drumming his fingers as Storm trotted around the perimeter of the paddock, sweeping right past them like a tease.

'We'll get to the bottom of it. I'm not worried yet. It just takes time.'

'Well, I admire your confidence,' she said, pulling her phone out to check the time. Ellie was supposed to be at the clinic by now, but she had called in sick, and there was a long list of animal patients still left to see today. A no-show was not ideal.

She looked up from the screen, feeling his eyes on her face. 'Everything OK?' he asked, sipping from the chipped mug, which by now was pretty much his mug. She had taken to arriving at the stables earlier than usual the last few mornings, just to have a coffee with him. It amused him whenever she kicked and cursed at the machine. The tension between them simmered just below the surface, a palpable undercurrent that seemed to charge the air with electricity every time there was a second of silence between them. Unless, of course, she was imagining it because of her dreams, and *he* hadn't noticed at all.

She explained that she was a little stressed because of her veterinary assistant's absence. 'Could it be something in his diet?' she then asked, steering the subject back to Storm so as not to appear entirely unprofessional. People got sick; it wasn't fair to be annoyed at the inconvenience.

Ethan nodded. 'It's possible. I've seen horses become more anxious when their feed is too high in sugar.'

'Exactly,' she said. 'Only, we've been careful what we fed him.'

Ethan shrugged. 'I doubt diet alone would cause such severe symptoms. I'd bet it's purely psychological but...'

'Until we can get close enough to rule anything out, we can't say for sure,' she finished, and he nodded, pulling out his shirt slightly. Even in the shade, it was hot, and she forced her eyes away from the fine chest hairs peeking out above the neckline. What was wrong with her? She almost wished he'd leave and take his sexy chest with him, but the mayor was paying for him to be here, and here he would stay until he succeeded.

Still, her wild dreams about him weren't helped by the fact that he was so good with the animals, when she'd actually assumed his so-called gift had been staged! He was also a good man in other ways, too. Ethan had rallied Billy to help repaint Lance's place, down at Redgum Ridge, once he knew the man had lost his wife. She knew she'd do well to keep things professional with Ethan, not to get too close, and definitely not let on how he was affecting her! The last time she'd let her barriers down with a man enough to truly make a connection—Bryce, ugh—he'd just disappeared on her, and while she most certainly was not going to be forging any kind of meaningful connection with Ethan in the brief time he was here, how could she not be intrigued by him?

Sage's thoughts drifted back to their conversation out on horseback the other day. She'd told him her parents died when she was ten, which in retrospect wasn't a whole lot of information, but the whole self-deprecating thing about being a weirdo who'd grown up talking to animals... Why had she said that? He was beyond perceptive. He could probably see by now that she was more than a little broken, but she'd gone and admitted her confidence, outside her veterinary skills, was in the toilet.

Still, why didn't he 'do' relationships? She was dying to ask him. Something about his tone and general secrecy had implied there was a pretty interesting reason behind that decision.

'I can help out,' Ethan said after a moment, his gaze not leaving Storm. 'I can't paint today anyway; Lance is expecting a delivery.'

Sage's heart kicked at her ribs. He would do that for her? Could she even handle working so closely with him?

'If you're sure,' she said nonchalantly, realising she sounded quite unsure of herself. He'd already moved in on her own responsibilities with Storm—not that she'd had a choice, and not that he wasn't making more progress than she ever had, annoyingly.

He turned to her, deadly serious, his voice low and gruff. 'Am I really so unconventional that you don't trust I'd obey your every command, Doctor?'

'I do trust you,' she heard herself say, a little too quickly. Gosh, why was she getting so hot again?

Later, Sage was wrapping up the last examination of the day—a cat who'd been struck down with the feline calicivirus—when she heard Ethan greeting someone who'd walked in. She would know that voice anywhere. Abigail, and her kids too by the sounds of it.

Waving off the lady and her cat, Sage felt unease coil in her belly as Abigail, gorgeous as ever in a long pink sundress, hair in a standard messy bun, raised her eyebrows out of Ethan's eyeline. Sage knew exactly what that look meant. It meant that Abigail also found him astonishingly attractive and was already pairing Sage up with him in her head!

'It's nice to meet Ethan here,' she said, beaming. 'I brought you some of that pineapple cake you like. Mum made too much again and you know it makes Daisy go doolally. Daisy, don't touch things, please, darling.'

Sure enough, Abigail was clutching her toddler, Charlie, over her bulging pregnant belly. Her five-year-old, Daisy, was already assessing the blue teddy bear in the box of toys by the window. Ethan crouched beside her, holding up a fire truck while throwing them both a look of his own that said he'd watch her a second.

'We should, uh, get this to the kitchen,' Abigail said loudly, holding up the cake tin. Quickly, Abigail pulled Sage by the sleeve towards the back room and shut the door. 'Oh, my God!' she murmured at her, eyes comically wide.

'Shh, Abi!'

'He's gorgeous!'

'He'll hear you!'

Abigail snorted and deposited Charlie onto the table, stretching out her back for a second before hoisting him back up onto her belly. 'So he's the one who's fixing our Storm?'

'Storm is not a car, Abi, but yeah, he's trying.'

'Maybe he can fix you too, if you know what I mean?' Abigail laughed and dodged Sage's play slap, then rummaged in the cupboard above the sink for mismatching plates. 'Seriously, the mayor didn't tell me he was this hot; I would've come by sooner.'

'I still think it's weird you call your own husband the mayor.' Sage sighed, slicing up the delicious-smelling cake, only just realising her stomach was growling. Abigail often fed her here when she worked long shifts, and the kids enjoyed meeting any animals she had in the healing room. Sometimes the thought sneaked in that some day she might like to have kids of her own. It wasn't entirely an unpleasant notion, the thought of raising a little animal-loving tribe to run around here with Abigail's, teaching them the ways of the world. A fresh start, she supposed.

Then she had to remind herself that in order to have kids, she'd actually have to meet a man… which meant opening herself up emotionally. Something she could never quite manage. Her life was the exact opposite of Abigail and the mayor's. It was so adorable how crazy they were about each other, how easy their relationship was. They trusted each other implicitly. When they bickered it always evolved into laughter. It felt inconceivable that she might some day find the same. There were things she probably shouldn't share with a man, and more that she couldn't laugh off. She'd never heard from Bryce again after he'd disappeared on her, and she'd liked him. A lot.

He'd shown up at the koala reserve, all smiles and stories, a bright light, a shiny distraction from Canada. He'd already done another three-month stint at an orangutan sanctuary in Borneo. A real nomad animal activist. They'd bonded, and for a while it had felt pretty real. More real than anything she'd known till then, at least. She'd slept with him, trusted him. He'd even promised to take her to Canada to meet his dog.

He'd vanished one morning. Left without so much as a 'this was nice but I'd better be on my way'. She'd always assumed he couldn't handle learning how and why her family had died. He'd looked horrified when she'd told him, literally the night before she'd found him gone! She'd taken the leap and confided in him, and straight away he'd brought the facts and newspaper articles about it up on his phone. As well as feeling wounded all over again by her parents' death, she'd had to relive the shame of hearing how many dead koalas the environmentalists had found in the following weeks. All the birds.

The story about the bushfire and her parents had done the rounds for months. She remembered her foster parents whispering about it, trying not to let on what they were talking about—but she'd grown to trust Bryce in their short time at the reserve. She'd revealed everything, the way she had disobeyed her parents' request that she leave her phone alone for a whole night while they got back to nature as a family and camped outdoors in their yard. She'd been such a stubborn ten-year-old, waiting till they fell asleep, then sneaking back into the house to grab her phone and text with her friends. She'd completely failed to notice that their smouldering fire was in danger of spreading into their makeshift camp. By the time she'd come back outside, the fire was raging beyond control. A neighbour had called the fire brigade, but it had been just…too late. The bush had burnt for a mile in all directions, taking her sleeping parents, their dog, and their tents with it. Sage had never forgiven herself.

'The mayor hired Ethan for up to six weeks,' Abigail commented now.

'Did he?' she said casually, forcing her focus back onto the cake. 'That's helpful. Ethan has offered to help me out while Ellie's off sick, too.' She realised from the look on Abi's face that, despite her efforts to appear unaffected, she must still sound quite put out about it.

'Listen to you! You sound like you don't want a stupidly handsome and incredibly buff guy walking around looking hot all day, helping you out.'

'I don't!'

'Liar.' Abigail took a huge bite of cake before Charlie swiped at it, sending it flying to the floor. 'Oh, God. Sorry, babe.'

'Leave it,' Sage told her, as the slice slid behind a floor cabinet. Charlie giggled in delight. 'Anyway, he might be hot, but it's not like he'd look twice at someone like me…a lonely spinster who spends most days hiding in a clinic in the middle of nowhere.'

Abigail cocked her head and scowled in the way she often applied to her kids. 'Stop that. You're a rock-star vet and a pillar of the community, Sage. Now, be a good spinster and deliver your hot new assistant some cake.'

Before Ethan could take his third bite of pineapple cake, having been accosted by Daisy and swept up in a game of teddy-bear-driving-fire-truck-over-cushions-and-books, the main phone shattered the playful reprise, during which Sage had firmly implanted the image of Ethan's future 'Greatest Dad' trophy in her brain. She answered the call, trying to ignore the looks Abigail kept shooting her whenever Ethan wasn't looking.

'Camel sanctuary?' she repeated. 'What's wrong with the camel?'

She could feel Ethan watching her intently throughout the call, his curiosity piqued as he finally got to finish his cake.

'OK,' she said, ending the call and looking up

at him. His eyes remained fixed on hers despite the blue teddy bear being swept across his head. 'There's a camel in distress at the sanctuary down by Cable Beach. They think it might be colic, but they aren't sure. Ellie's still out sick, obviously, so I'll be going alone.'

'Why don't I come with you?' Ethan offered, oblivious to Abigail pulling another dramatic face behind him as she swept up the toys and ushered Daisy through the door, waving goodbye.

'No, thank you, I'll be fine,' she said.

'I've dealt with colic before, and it might be good for you to have a second opinion.'

'Are you sure?' Sage asked, realising she didn't actually have a good reason to refuse him, even though she really could have done with some distance to fight this mounting and deeply unsettling attraction. 'It's been a long day already, and I don't want to impose.'

Ethan just stood with his empty plate, then deposited it dutifully back into the kitchen. 'We should get going,' he called back. 'My ute, or yours?'

CHAPTER SIX

'PRETTY INTERESTING PLACE, isn't it?' Sage remarked, feeling her boots sinking into the soft white sand outside Camel Ride HQ. The afternoon heat shimmered over the beach ahead of them, casting an almost ethereal glow over the surroundings.

'Emphasis on the pretty,' Ethan replied, glancing at her quickly—too quickly to know if he was referring to her or not—before taking in the scene with a mixture of curiosity and amusement. They could already see people on camels, heading out from HQ onto the sand. This company ran tours all day, every day, as well as rescuing camels and orphaned calves and giving them a new loving home.

As he joined her on the path from the parking lot, she picked up on his scent again, the earthy musk of it, almost animal. He hadn't had to join her out here, but he'd volunteered, which felt more exciting than it should; this was getting silly now. Abigail had got into her head too. As if anything was going to happen outside her hot, sweaty dreams.

'Dr Dawson!' A woman in an orange skirt with long strawberry-blonde hair pulled back in a ponytail was holding her hand up, exiting the main building ahead. This was Marleen, the woman who'd called her. Soon they were both being ushered into the long corrugated-iron shed, where twenty or so stalls were bulging with hay and healthy-looking camels. A small crowd was already gathered around one of the enclosures, which Marleen dismissed as they approached. The camel was lying on the ground, its breathing laboured and shallow. Ethan got to his knees in his jeans, back muscles flexed as he murmured to the sick animal, rolling up his sleeves.

The poor creature looked so vulnerable and helpless. It stirred a wellspring of empathy inside her as she knelt beside Ethan with the stethoscope, running her fingers gently along the camel's side. The soft groaning sound the creature made caused her heart to ache as Ethan gently lifted its heavy head, his strong hands cradling it with tenderness.

'Could be dehydration, or even anaemia,' he suggested, and she pressed her fingers to the camel's neck next, feeling for any swollen lymph nodes. The scent of hay and animal musk hung heavily in the air, mingling with the salty breeze drifting in from nearby Cable Beach, and Ethan's scent too. She couldn't get enough of it. He was close now, leaning even closer, feeling along the camel's back as she ran the stethoscope over the smooth fur of the creature's belly and sides. Sage couldn't help but steal glances at him as he concentrated, admiring his strong hands and the way the sunlight was streaming in through the door and dancing off his dark hair.

'Her gums are pale,' Ethan said after a moment. He was peering into the camel's mouth now.

'And her heart rate is elevated,' Sage confirmed. 'Anaemia seems unlikely though, given her diet and environment. She doesn't appear to have any external wounds or lesions.'

Ethan reached for the thermometer and she watched as he slipped it under the camel's tongue. She could feel the animal tremble beneath her touch.

'Temperature's normal,' he announced after a moment, his brow furrowed in concentration. Then he pressed his ear to the creature's neck. He appeared to be listening intently as if trying to discern some other subtle clue from the animal's laboured breaths and she wondered…did this gift he had with horses extend to other animals?

'We'll run some blood tests,' she said to him, worried for a moment that she might be starting to believe he could diagnose an animal without any modern tools at all. He helped her collect the samples, she asked Marleen a few more standard questions and arranged some pain meds, while Ethan mumbled something indecipherable to the camel, still stroking her tenderly. By the time they left the stall, the poor thing was definitely calmer.

On the way out, Ethan stopped promptly at another stall, where a smaller camel was grazing. The gentle creature looked up, focusing its doe eyes on him. Then, to Sage's surprise, it stepped forward and promptly placed its head in Ethan's waiting hands.

What is happening?

Ethan seemed to study the camel in silence, caressing its big soft head, before a smile flashed across his lips. 'I think she's pregnant,' he announced.

Marleen, who was watching in equal fascination, shook her head. 'Nah, mate. No way. We just got her—she's a newbie.'

'It happened before she got here,' Ethan murmured. Sage felt her pulse fire up as he guided her hand to the camel's belly, his warm fingers lingering just a moment too long on hers. 'Do you feel that?'

'Is that…a heartbeat?' Sage looked at him in shock as she felt the unmistakable rhythm of life beneath her fingertips. 'Ethan, you're right.' A quick exam with her stethoscope proved it.

'Really?' Marleen looked confused as he showed her how to feel for the heartbeat, too, without the stethoscope. 'But she's not even showing. How did you know?'

Ethan just shrugged his shoulders and dragged a hand through his hair. It was loose now, free of its usual ponytail, and Sage had to admit she really liked it. It looked wild. Marleen was looking at him in awe. 'How…?'

'It's a gift,' Sage heard herself whisper.

Marleen's eyes widened.

Of course, Sage had looked all this up online, and there were lots of animal communicators out there, lots of proven cases of people diagnosing mystery problems. It still didn't make it any more conceivable to her scientific brain…but it was definitely hot when Ethan did it. She'd known, since before he even drove onto her dusty forecourt, that he had a special gift with horses, but to see it *did* in fact appear to transfer to other animals actually left her speechless.

It wasn't right to feel jealous of him. This was not a competition. But she'd had to work so hard for her qualifications and here Ethan Matthews was, doing everything as easily as breathing. Her envy was quickly merging with admiration, however, the more she witnessed him in action. The attraction she felt to him in this moment was so far off the charts there was hardly a measure for it, she thought, forcing her feet to walk her back outside while Ethan and Marleen discussed the pregnancy. What if he could see inside her head, too? Lord, the shame of what he'd see!

He found her by the ute, watching the ocean. Its gentle lulling waves, the sound of the gulls, all of it was a balm to her frazzled senses.

'Marleen asked us to join the sunset camel safari.' Ethan opened the door and dropped the bag back onto the back seat. 'I said I'd ask you. Are you as confident on camels as you are on horses?'

'They don't tend to move as fast,' she replied coolly, instantly aware of his manly presence beside her; the way her skin and cells stood to attention. 'Sure, we can ride, if you like.'

On the beach, Marleen and her staff were greeting the returning riders and guiding the camels to water. They'd have to wait a few minutes for their turn. The ocean glistened and a fishing boat bobbed in a path of sparkles as she dropped to the sand, letting the warmth travel up through her feet to her bones.

'This reminds me of my dad,' she said aloud without thinking. 'We used to visit the ocean a lot when I was little.'

Ethan was quiet a moment as they studied the sky on the horizon. The sun was already sinking, a huge ball of fire casting peach-amber streaks across the water. 'Losing your parents, at just ten years old, I can't imagine. What happened to you after that?'

'I got lucky,' she said, turning to him. 'I landed

on the *good* side of the foster system. Ken and Arielle treated me like their real daughter, and I love them like one. But you never forget a loss like that. It only takes a little thing, like this view, or a smell, or a song to bring it all back.'

'I know,' he said on a deep exhale that came right from his heart. Of course he knew.

'Were you close with your mum?' she asked.

'Very.'

She bit her lip. There were so many questions she wanted to ask him, still, but he wasn't staying long, and the last thing she should be doing was sharing her feelings, or catching more feelings for someone who'd simply disappear back into the TV in a few weeks...or wherever else he was called to next.

Soon, the sunset tour group was gathered on the sand, and Marleen had Ethan stepping on a small stepladder up to the seat on the camel, which made Sage laugh. Just the way the bulky beige animal lowered to its knobbly knees to let the equally awkward humans on its back was hilarious.

'You next,' Marleen said, gesturing to her. Sage paused. Oh, so they were riding in twos, on the same camel?

OK, then.

Ethan held out his hand and she clasped it tight, allowing him to hoist her up into the seat. She sat in front, with barely a centimetre between her back and his chest, just like the other 'couples' in the group. Maybe Marleen had misinterpreted their relationship…not that she was complaining, exactly.

Just enjoy it for what it is, she told herself, settling into his safe, strong proximity, letting out a thrilled shriek as their camel stood up slowly, as if it was actually being careful not to drop its heavy load.

Ethan's hands landed on her shoulders, steadying her. He kept them there as he pointed at a young couple attempting to coax a stubborn camel into posing for a photo further down the beach. As the sun dipped lower in the sky, painting the horizon and people with deeper shades of orange, Sage found herself relaxing, even though the camel's plod was bumpier than any horse she'd ever ridden. Every now and then her back would brush Ethan's chest and sparks of adrenaline flooded her belly from behind. The salty breeze tugged at their hair and hers was more than likely landing in his mouth from time to time, but he wasn't complaining. Was it weird that she'd never ridden a camel before? She was just about to ask Ethan this question when he spoke over her shoulder.

'You know, I haven't been to the beach in a long time.'

She swivelled her head back to him and bumped his nose with hers by mistake. He laughed, as did she, but his eyes quickly fixed on the setting sun. He'd felt it too—when their noses touched—and he clearly didn't want to address it.

'Why not?' she said, feeling a flash of heat to her groin as her back slid another couple of times against his torso. She should focus on the magnificent view, but the effects of Ethan's muscles swiping her flesh with just flimsy bits of material between them were impossible to ignore.

'I had a pretty big bust-up with a good friend on the beach not so long ago and it brings it all back.' He stopped talking abruptly, his mouth a thin line. Sage's heart was already hammering. She knew she shouldn't ask but it was way too intriguing. This was more than he'd ever said about his life.

'A bust-up?'

'More like a heated argument.'

'What about?' she dared to press. He didn't seem the type to engage in arguments of any kind. But Ethan stayed silent. Then he sighed so hard she felt it ripple through her hair, leaving a trail of goosebumps on the back of her neck.

'You don't even want to know,' he said, finally. His tone silenced her, right until their group came to a stop and they were ordered to dismount for a break and a drink. This was more vulnerability than she'd expected from some supposedly arrogant hotshot celebrity vet. Maybe she'd painted him as that quite unfairly. It was becoming clearer every day that there was more to Ethan Matthews than she'd seen…maybe more than anyone watching him on TV had ever seen. He had layers, and some of those were still tender, still painful, as hers were. She was so caught up in her thoughts about his mysterious bust-up on the beach that she almost missed what was going on around her.

Oh, no.

Already, everyone was settling down around a huge, spitting, burning, roaring fire.

CHAPTER SEVEN

SAGE SLID OFF the camel after Ethan and stepped onto the sand, inhaling air deeply into her lungs. Their guide was handing out small cups filled with sweet tea and she took one gratefully, breathing in the aromatic scent; anything for a distraction. Ethan was taking a seat close to the fire already, where someone had scattered cushions in anticipation of the tour group. This was basic tourist stuff, and she willed herself to calm down as laughter and conversation filled the air, along with the giant sparks from the crackling logs and driftwood.

Don't be a baby. Don't be an idiot, Sage.

Despite her internal pep talk, fear and panic welled up inside her as she closed her eyes. The memories were slamming her now from all directions. Her cup almost crumpled in her fierce grip. She'd stood just like this that night, helplessly overwhelmed in front of the raging bushfire, watching the tents ablaze beyond a flaming row of bushes. She'd stared, unable to move, feet glued to the floor. It was only when the neighbour had arrived and swept her up in his arms and carried her away that she'd been able to comprehend the magnitude of what had happened, what she'd failed to try and prevent, but by then, everything was gone. Everyone had died.

'Sage?'

Ethan was in front of her suddenly. His curious gaze made her shuffle in embarrassment as he studied her distance from the fire. 'What's wrong? Don't you want to sit closer?'

'No, I'm fine here,' she replied, her heart pounding in her chest at the thought of revealing her vulnerability to him, as she had to Bryce. 'I just, uh, I don't like fire a lot. At all.'

'You don't like *fire*?'

She would have to say something. 'There was a bushfire,' she said finally. 'Around our property. That's how I lost my parents.'

Ethan was quiet. Maybe it was the fact that she'd sensed his own vulnerability back there, about the argument with his friend, that had forced her guard down just a little, but his eyes were filled with such empathy and sadness now, she almost felt sick.

'I lost my dog that night, too,' she added. Might as well get it all out. In fact, she was quite prepared to carry on, suddenly, to tell him everything about how she'd failed to save them all, how the fire had spread beyond control past their little makeshift campsite, designed to get the family back to nature and away from all technology for the night, how the house had burned to the ground next along with all their possessions, but her voice got lodged in her windpipe till she could barely breathe, let alone speak.

'Sage.' Ethan was looking at her with such horror now, she was glad she'd stopped talking. 'What happened?' he asked. 'I mean, how did you—?'

'I still think about Juni, my dog,' she interrupted, nervously. 'Maybe that's why I do what I do, you know? If I can save just one animal's life, then I can still make a difference.'

'You make a big difference here every day, everyone knows that,' he said. 'But, Sage, I'm so sorry to hear about your family.'

'Doesn't matter. Enough about me, what about you, Mr Secretive? What was your big argument with your friend about? Does that have anything to do with why you don't *do* relationships?'

Her blurted questions hung in the air like a lead balloon. The laughter around them seemed to fade into the background as her heart slammed in her chest. Abigail would have punched her in the arm right about now; that eager question made her seem way too interested in deep diving into his life history than was acceptable, or attractive, but better to talk about him than her, and all the stuff that she couldn't discuss.

Ethan's eyes met hers again and she swallowed. Suddenly she forgot what she'd been thinking. There it was, plain as day: layers of hesitation and discomfort flickering within their ocean-blue depths. She'd hit the nail on the head. Whatever had happened on that beach was exactly why he didn't do relationships. Taking a step back again, she watched the group over the rim of her cup, desperate for some distance between herself and this burning reminder of her own trauma, and the feel of his eyes burning equally hot on her face.

'I'll get us some cushions,' he said, and she wrestled with the guilt as she watched him collect two from beside the fire, his muscular frame a solid silhouette against the flames and the fading sun. He motioned for her to take a seat beside him away from the flames, and watched her closely, as if she might combust with her grief.

'You sure this is OK?' he asked.

'I'm fine here,' she replied. 'So, you were saying?'

He shook his head and adjusted himself on the cushion. 'It's…complicated,' he muttered as she put down her cup.

'Isn't it always?' she said. It felt as if her cheeks had absorbed the flames as he took her in, as if committing her freckles to memory. Then he cleared his throat and dropped back onto the sand, resting back on one thick, toned arm. The firelight played on the rock of his biceps, a thin sheen of sweat making her lick her lips despite herself. Maybe fire wasn't so bad under the right circumstances. She was fully attuned to him now, and there was no way he didn't feel the same; the air between them was buzzing, even though he was clearly deflecting. Something complicated had stomped on any wish he might have once had for a relationship with someone special and he didn't want to talk about it.

'Look, I didn't mean to make you uncomfortable,' she said softly, hoping her eyes were filled with sincerity as much as the questions that were still jumping about in her brain. 'I understand if it's something you don't want to talk about. I know what that's like.'

Ethan pressed his lips together a moment. 'You're right, I don't normally talk about this stuff with anyone.' His voice was strained with the effort to find the right words. 'I was with someone for a long time. We were engaged to be married, and I very much *wanted* to be in that relationship with Carrie, until she...'

Carrie?

Sage gripped his hand without thinking, feeling the warmth of his skin beneath her fingertips instantly. 'Oh, no, Ethan. Did Carrie die?'

Ethan's eyes grew wide. Mortified for him, she squeezed his hand. It should have been obvious, of course, the pain she'd seen in his eyes, the way he was reluctant to talk about it, just as she still was. It hurt too much. It would always hurt.

'No one died,' he blurted, biting back a humourless laugh.

'Oh. Sorry.' Sage pulled her hands away and hugged her knees to her chest. Great, now he thought she was a total drama queen. 'I just always assume…'

'No one actually died,' he said again, gruffly. 'But I have two people in my life who are pretty much dead to me now and maybe that's the saddest thing about what happened. I miss them even though they're still alive. I miss what we all used to be to one another. We won't ever be that way again.'

'What did they do? I assume the one who isn't Carrie is the person you argued with.'

'On the beach, yes. Palm Cove to be exact,' he finished. 'His name's Cam.' The name came out through slightly clenched teeth before he continued. 'Cameron. I've known him my whole life, since we started school together.'

Sage realised she was staring at him with her mouth open as the pieces started fitting together in her head. Ethan had been engaged once, and then his fiancée did something, and now there were two people he couldn't see. Cam was one. What did his buddy Cam do to cause a bust-up…? Oh, no. He'd stolen Ethan's fiancée! She knew it without him saying; it was written all over his face.

'They're married now,' he confirmed, still looking at the fire. She shook her head, touching a hand to his quickly as he sat back up beside her, cross-legged. 'I hear it was a beautiful wedding.'

Sage pulled a face, and he mirrored it. 'Look at us,' he said, wrinkling his nose. 'We only came to help a camel, and now we're on a beach, which I hate, near a fire, which you hate—'

'Well, at least we're alive.' She smiled, nudging his shoulder with hers. 'And beaches aren't that bad, are they?'

'Not when you're with me, they aren't.' Sage felt the shivers from her fingers right through to her feet as he took her hand and held it tight over his knee. 'I like talking to you, Doctor,' he murmured, without realising he was stealing all the breath from her body.

'How long were you together?' she asked as the heat of his hand seared through her, hotter than the fire.

'A long time,' he replied, looking at their fingers. 'Seven years.'

'And how long ago did you split up?'

'Thirteen months ago. That's when I found out about it anyway.'

'Some friend,' she heard herself say, before she could hold it in. The injustice of it all left a nasty taste in her mouth, and a tsunami of empathy for him threatened to have her say more, but she didn't, equally occupied by the drumbeat throb of her heart now that he was holding her hand. Even as their group reassembled around them, ready for the ride back up the beach, Sage felt suspended by some strange new gravity holding her right here.

So she'd had a messed-up start herself as a ten-year-old orphaned girl, but at least no one had betrayed her as Ethan had been betrayed; not that she'd let anyone close enough to try. She'd started to think she wouldn't know how to be someone's long-term partner anyway, that maybe it just wasn't in her destiny. At the heart of it, she supposed—and as Abigail often reminded her— was her raging guilt. It slammed shut every door she'd ever tried to open, till she'd eventually given up. Why should she be happy when her family never would be again, because of her selfishness?

The silence between them grew heavier, punctuated only by the sounds of the camels' footsteps and the distant laughter of the other riders. The sun had fully sunk now, but the moon was huge and the magnetic pull from Ethan only seemed to intensify every time he looked her way. It didn't subside in the ute either. The whole way back to Amber Creek, it felt a lot as if an unspoken desire to unpick the other's past was simmering between them. Unless it was all her, she considered, stealing another glance at his profile in the moonlight.

What was his ex-fiancée like? Was she pretty? Of *course* she was pretty. Ethan wouldn't have been with anyone *not* pretty for all those years.

'Look,' Ethan said suddenly, gesturing towards the paddock. They were back at the clinic already, where they'd planned for him to drop her off before he drove on back to the guest house. She turned to where he was pointing, but he was sprinting from the ute already, making for the gate. Sage's heart swelled as she watched him vault over it with one leap again.

A momentary reprieve from the intensity of her thoughts was promptly replaced by slight alarm. Storm was lying down in the grass, cool as a cucumber under the moon, calmer than she'd ever seen him. He was lying right next to Karma and, contrary to all of their previous encounters, the two horses seemed entirely comfortable with each other.

She gasped as she reached the gate and watched Ethan kneel slowly in front of them. Karma snorted and got to his feet, trotting off merrily, but Storm, to her total surprise, stayed put, and lowered his head, as if bowing to him. Even from where she was, she could tell that this was progress. Storm had never been this welcoming or appeared this placid before, and he barely flinched as Ethan started running his hands gently along his neck and back.

'He's going to let me examine him,' Ethan said,

and the look of victory on his face made her grin, it was so infectious. 'I'll wait till the morning, first light,' he followed, striding back over to her. He met her on the other side of the gate.

'It was only a matter of time,' she heard herself say, through her own smile. Why did he have to be so gorgeous, on top of being a bona fide equine wizard?

Maybe it was having the gate safely between them, but a quiet confidence overruled her common sense. Before she knew it, her fingers were reaching out for his face, brushing off a small fleck of ash from his left cheek that had been bugging her since the beach. He caught her fingers deftly, and held them against his face, and for a moment neither of them moved as he scanned her eyes. An almost tortured expression hovered in his gaze that made her pulse thud, before he reached across the gate and cupped the back of her neck. Butterflies exploded in her belly.

Oh, my Lord...he's going to kiss me.

Sage closed her eyes and prepared herself as her heart started bucking like an unbroken horse in her chest.

Don't move, she willed herself. *You do deserve this, just one kiss. One little kiss to keep you floating from someone who's just passing through. That would be OK, wouldn't it? That would be enough.*

He was inching closer over the gate, she could

feel his breath warming her face, smell his earthy scent mingling with heat and hay. He was going to kiss her, she knew it. Any second now...

Ethan pressed his lips to her cheek, and then dropped her hand. In a beat he scaled the gate, landing with a thud beside her as she blinked her eyes back open, mortified.

Her senses screamed in unison—*What about the kiss? The proper kiss!*

'I should go. We have an early start tomorrow,' he said, striding ahead of her towards the car.

Reeling, Sage hugged her arms tightly around herself as he gave her a final look over his shoulder, then drove away. OK...so that was weird, she thought, straightening up and composing herself. They'd been so close to kissing, but he'd backed off. Probably for the best, she thought with a wince, seeing as there was no point starting up anything with someone who was leaving as soon as Storm's issues were fixed, but still... hmm. Something must have been going through his mind to have pulled away like that, though. Was it Carrie? She frowned down the drive, now devoid of any sign of him. Perhaps he wasn't over Carrie.

CHAPTER EIGHT

ETHAN KEPT HIS hands steady as he aligned the splint against the koala's fragile leg. All the while his heart thrummed an erratic beat that betrayed the calm of his practised movements. Sage was close, too close, her own hands mirroring his with a deftness that spoke volumes about her compassion and skill, both of which he'd had the pleasure, and the torture, of observing up close since volunteering to help her out at the clinic. He'd almost pressed his mouth to hers last week. What the hell was wrong with him?

Ellie had come in briefly to share some patient files, despite her sickness, and before Sage had sent her away again to rest she had eyed him in that usual awestruck way. He was used to women like her, looking at him as if he were something amazing, something to be devoured with a gaze alone.

A woman like Sage, however, who grasped at the broken shards of his soul and loosened the reins on his heart, and made him want to talk about things he would rather usually not talk about…that was something else entirely. He had never felt so drawn to anyone so inexplicably before. It was as if her wounded soul called out to him—and it was why he'd almost kissed her. But also why he'd swiftly backed off. There was no way he was going down the road Carrie had taken him on again, where a woman had bent his universe so out of shape that the loss had altered his DNA for ever.

Still, with Ellie still sick, here he was. How could he have kept his distance knowing they were running out of hands to attend to all these animals? There was so much to do. And now that Storm was finally responding to him without galloping off a mile each time, it was imperative he stay close, vital he make sure the horse didn't do a one-eighty and backtrack on the progress he'd made in the week since conducting that first physical exam.

'Good, just like that,' Sage murmured now, her voice soft but authoritative as she secured the bandage. The air between them was charged, thick with the words they hadn't spoken since that…what had it been? A mistake. It *should* have felt like a mistake, but every time he watched her mouth move now, the slow burn for her went from a smoulder to a full-on inferno till all he could think about was pressing Sage Dawson up against the stable wall, running his hands over

the curve of her hips and claiming her lips and…
healing her, like one of his horses? As if he could.
He hadn't even been able to heal *himself* enough
after his mother had died to notice Carrie was
slipping away.

'Ethan?'

'Yeah, it's secure,' he said.

Focus, man. What was it now, just seven days?
A week of wondering if he just should've kissed
her and been done with it.

Ethan kept his attention on the tasks at hand,
trying to ignore how the scent of her—wildflowers and something uniquely Sage—overwhelmed
his senses. His ego didn't quite know how to handle looking in a mirror like this, seeing someone
else so fragile, someone else he didn't know how
to fix. She'd been keeping her distance, too.

'Steady there, mate, we're almost done,' he
whispered to the fidgeting koala, who blinked
up at them with trusting, glassy eyes. The animal's quiet resilience struck a chord with him. In
the face of its obvious pain, it was clearly letting
them help. If only his own efforts to maintain his
composure weren't so flimsy around Sage. Every
time he so much as brushed against her acciden-
tally, that moment in the paddock the other night
flew back into his brain, as well as the way he'd
exited stage left as if she'd threatened him with
a cattle prod!

But after everything he'd spilled to her on the

beach, after showing that level of vulnerability it was hard to place the feelings he was starting to experience for someone who didn't even live in the same Australian territory as him. Why start up anything with someone like her, who'd be incredibly hard to get over? The dreams he was having were torture enough.

He used to have regular dreams about walking in on Cam with Carrie. They had tortured him for months, and he'd barely dared to think about sex as anything other than something *they* were doing together, which had repulsed him. Now, though, his suddenly revived libido was roaring back in spades, taking those dreams to new places, mostly steamy midnight rides with Sage, and not always on horseback...

Sage stood back, running a gentle hand over their brave koala. 'Thank you, Ethan,' she said on a sigh, brushing a wisp of hair from her forehead. 'I couldn't have done this without you. We're so short-staffed.'

Ever the professional attitude now, he mused.

'Any time,' he replied gruffly as she snatched her gaze away again and turned to the sink, visibly flustered by his closeness. She'd told him some pretty personal things on the beach, and he'd reciprocated. At least, he'd told her the necessary details. And then he'd turned away from her. She hadn't brought it up since, or the almost kiss, and neither had he, but it still hung between them in the silence.

'What's next for today?' Sage's question cut through his inner reverie.

'I'm just thinking about Storm out there,' he lied, offering a tight smile. He *should* be thinking about Storm—he and Billy were planning to try and saddle him later—but now he was thinking about Sage, yet again.

'He's already doing so much better; the mayor said so this morning, didn't he?' she said, before going on to the subject of the new food and troughs Ethan had suggested, and then the weather. Her brow creased slightly, and she diverted her eyes the whole time, as if she was just filling the air with words for the sake of saying something, anything. He watched her shift the koala gently on the table, motioning for him to open the cage. 'Could you bring it a little closer?' she said.

Ethan picked it up easily and placed it closer. Her sleeve caught for a second on the cage door, and he freed her deftly, then drew his hand back quickly this time, before she could retreat from him again. 'Sorry,' they both muttered simultaneously. Then they shared an awkward smile over the koala's head. Why did he feel like a fake all of a sudden? As if he was lying about not wanting to rip off her clothes, press his mouth to hers and kick the door shut behind them.

'Looks like our friend will be OK,' he said about the koala. It seemed to be quite comfortable now, if a little dozy.

'We're a good team,' Sage replied. More words to fill the silence, from both of them this time. Then she busied herself folding up some towels while he filled in the animal's file. The little marsupial's leg was neatly splinted now. She was right, their team was a good one for the most part. He watched her cross the room, putting significant distance between them again as she put away instruments and bottles.

'What?' she said, somewhat nervously from near the window, brushing another tuft of fallen hair from her eyes.

The air between them was charged with that thick, hot, electric buzz he knew should be defused. Every rational thought screamed at him to keep his distance, yet his hands and his body seemed entirely disinclined to obey right now. Sage was the first person who'd made him forget the extent of the pain Carrie and Cam had inflicted on him, but at the same time, this thing had just as much potential to mess with his head, more than it already was. Talk about being blindsided! The very last thing he'd expected to find when accepting this gig was a woman like Sage bringing his libido back to life, most inappropriately!

'What?' she said again as he looked at her. She

sounded so conflicted, as though his eyes on her made her feel things she didn't know what to do with. Same as him, then.

'You…' he started.

Sage lowered her head slightly, then looked up at him through her eyelashes. This mad chemistry was not going to go away. Maybe he should just address it? Drag it out into the open so they could laugh about it.

As if he would laugh about it.

'Me?' she said, finally, searching his face through narrowed green eyes.

He opened his mouth. The words formed on his tongue: *You are driving me crazy.*

He stepped forwards, all efforts to resist this gone, out of the window.

As if on cue, the shrill ring of the clinic's phone shattered the bubble. Sage cleared her throat, lifting the receiver. 'This is Dr Dawson.'

The caller's frantic voice spilled through the line; something about a bird, rare and injured, found miles away. With each detail, Ethan's professional focus snapped back into place. What was he thinking, almost letting that craziness consume him again?

'Got it. We're on it.' Sage hung up and turned to him, her expression grave. 'It's a black-throated finch. Someone up at Koorabimby Nook's found one, but it's badly hurt.'

Ethan frowned. He had no clue where Koorabimby Nook was, but the black-throated finch species was in a precarious state, almost extinct, in fact.

'What's the plan?' he asked, and she bit her bottom lip thoughtfully, pacing the room while the koala looked on.

'It's too far by road. We won't make it in time,' she calculated quickly, making his mind race through alternatives. But Sage was already on the phone again, dialling someone.

'Mayor Warragul, it's Sage Dawson. We've got a situation with a black-throated finch,' she said. 'I need a huge favour.'

Ethan watched, admiration warming his chest as they talked. Her decisiveness was one of the hundreds of things he admired about her—her ability to switch modes and take action under pressure, her drive to save any creature, no matter the odds. It had started with losing her dog, she'd told him that, which made sense if it died in the bushfire, but there was so much he didn't know; not that he would be asking. Getting too personal had never been part of his plan when he got here… In fact he'd made up his mind to get the job with Storm done as fast as he could and get back to rebuilding the second beehive with Dad, the one his niece and nephew wanted to keep as their own. And he was losing his train of thought about what mattered most, more often than was safe. He'd almost kissed Sage already. Twice.

'We should pack a field kit,' she said now, and he helped her gather supplies.

'How are we going to get there?' he asked her on their way out. He'd failed to hear exactly how Amber Creek's mayor was planning to help them in this situation.

Sage turned to him, her expression a blend of determination and hope. 'The mayor's going to fly us out there in his chopper.'

The whirr of the helicopter blades grew louder as they approached, the rhythmic chopping sound slicing through the air.

'Thanks for doing this, Mayor,' Sage said as they climbed aboard, her voice barely audible over the din. Ethan watched them make brief conversation, admiring this multifaceted mayor who clearly had a soft spot for Sage. She'd been close with his wife Abigail since she moved here, he remembered as the helicopter lifted off and Billy and the horses and Sage's rock garden grew smaller and smaller below. In fact, Sage had been to their house a few times since he'd joined their small team at the clinic. They loved her, and she loved those kids. It was nice to see. He wasn't so great with kids himself, with the exception of Jacqueline's kids, Kara and Jayson—the horses had always been easier to understand, and quieter too—but sometimes he imagined a tribe of his own: little people who he could teach to ride and read and take over the plot some day. Carrie had wanted all that, initially. She'd probably get it too, with Cam.

'I hope we're not too late,' he heard Sage say, and he stopped himself saying anything. There was no point in giving her false hope. Who knew the extent of the bird's injuries? It was moments like these, however, that reminded him why he'd become a veterinarian himself—to save and protect animals in their natural environment, to give a voice to the creatures who couldn't speak for themselves. The rare finch had been mentioned in a lecture at a conference, just the other month, about endangered species, and now here he was, with Sage in a chopper, on a mission to save one. Dad would get a kick out of this story.

Sage sat next to him now, her face pressed against the window as she scanned the terrain below. Her eyes filled with concern, and maybe a little annoyance too as the massive coal mines started dominating the landscape below. The stark contrast between the untouched wilderness and industrialisation was even more unsettling from up here. So many creatures had perished and would perish with all this overdevelopment. It only strengthened his resolve to do everything in his power to protect and preserve this fragile ecosystem, as well as get the homestead running as sustainably as they could back in Queensland.

He found himself staring at her mouth, thinking again about their almost-kiss, when she turned to him and found his eyes on her. It was too late to turn away. Busted. She quirked an eyebrow and shook her head.

'It's not a good idea, Ethan,' she murmured over the rotors. Ethan's pulse spiked but he kept his expression in neutral.

'What isn't?'

'You know what,' she said, sweeping her hair back to a rough ponytail and holding it to the nape of her neck, like his. He said nothing; what could he say? It was not a good idea, and of course he knew it.

She released her hair, letting the chestnut waves loose till they were catching the gusts from the open door and billowing around her face. Wild strands whipped against his cheek, daring him to question the validity of these claims.

Oh, so that's how she's playing this.

She was freaking out, because, yes, it had almost happened again, and she knew it shouldn't because they were colleagues? Who knew why, really? But she was making excuses. She wanted him as much as he wanted her. Just by saying *this* she was confirming it. He couldn't fight the smile from his mouth at the look of pure tortured desire in her eyes.

'Stop it,' she said again, pretending to thump his shoulder.

'Stop what?'

'Looking at me like…that.'

Then her face seemed to scrunch up in front of him before she pressed her face into her hands quickly, as if she was trying to erase her last words. 'I shouldn't have said anything, should I? You weren't going to. Forget I said anything?'

'I can barely hear you anyway,' he lied loudly, pointing at the roof, mouthing, *The blades are too loud*.

She pulled another face and shook her head at the window, and he busied himself with double-checking the contents of the field kit, pulling it between them on the seat, creating a necessary distance between them. OK…so the small talk was killing him, but if she thought him kissing her for any reason was a bad idea, he'd respect that, of course. He was here to work, after all. There was no point getting swept up in this… thing. She'd obviously been thinking about their situation as much as he had, so much in fact that she'd blurted out an attempt at resistance, to push him away. He almost asked her why she'd done it, but did it matter, in the end? What could come of it? Best to keep things professional, however hard it was going to be.

The noise of the chopper felt like a fitting match for the turmoil he could feel building inside him though, every time he considered how much he was kidding himself, trying to imagine it would be fine for the rest of his time here ignoring the obvious sexual tension between them. They should talk about this. It would hang over them otherwise. He'd promised to work the weekend on the drip irrigation system outside her house and she'd agreed. Why had she done that, if she didn't want him getting too close?

She wasn't looking at him now, she was talking to the mayor again, and he weighed up his options, watching the curve of her shoulders in her billowing white shirt. He could simply tell her there was no room in his life for romance either. In truth it wasn't what he was looking for at all, at least, not a *relationship*. But anything else would end badly, not just because of the distance between their home lives. He could never leave Dad, and the horses, and all of Mum's memories, the same as she could never leave her practice. This was probably just his libido rebooting after months of being dead and dormant, that was all.

Also, Carrie and Cam had a point. His work would always come first, he would always be considered a solitary enigma, and any good self-respecting woman would tire of that eventually, as Carrie had. And Sage's life was here. It was hard to measure how much he admired her for pulling her life together, for providing this selfless service to others. How could anyone go through losing both their parents in a bushfire and come out so strong and seemingly self-assured?

On the *outside*, he reminded himself quickly. Sage appeared strong on the outside, to most people. But now she was showing him her vulnerabilities too. He was one of them. For that reason, he would stay well away from her.

'It's over here!' The towering, big-built lady in knee-high rubber boots raised a trowel at them as they reached the path, metres from the chopper. The mayor had landed in a eucalyptus field and Ethan noted the Koorabimby Nook sign by the slatted house. Ah, so it was part of a farm. Llamas and a solo horse were looking at them curiously. There, beneath a scrubby bush, lay the finch, its delicate plumage ruffled, one bloodied wing hanging at an unnatural angle. They crouched down beside it and Sage held a hand up, instantly protective of the rare bird.

'Careful,' she instructed, as if she needed to, as he gently scooped up the injured creature, cradling it in his big hands. Blood soaked his fingers. Sage's gaze turned sad. 'It doesn't look good,' she told him. She was right, it didn't. Some kind of animal attack? It was definitely a predator of some sort that had done this much damage.

'I think it probably had a disagreement with a cat,' Sage said with a frown, confirming his thoughts.

'I think he had a run-in with one of mine, yes,' the woman told them sadly, blocking the sun from their faces with her generous frame. Sage communicated her sorrow with him via another look, her fingers gently probing as he held the bird steady. It was hot, still, in the afternoon sun. Its low-hanging intensity scorched the back of his neck as he watched a bead of sweat trail down Sage's cheek. Why did he want to touch her so badly, even in moments like this? It was completely unprofessional and unnecessary, and it was damn well not helping his resolve to keep his emotions out of working with her.

'Fractured wing, possible internal injuries,' Sage was noting now. 'We'll get some pain meds ready. We can't do a proper analysis until we get it to the clinic.'

'Will it survive that long?' the woman asked in concern. 'They're rare, you know.'

'We know,' Sage said after a lingering pause, flashing her eyes to his. Ethan got the distinct impression she wanted to tell the woman to lock up her cats. There wasn't much you could do about natural instinct, though. He should know; his was building the longer those beads of sweat trickled down Sage's cheek…and onto her neck. All he wanted was to touch her, wipe them away with his lips, as if that were likely to cool her down. Or him.

Back in the chopper, the mayor was ready to

take off the second they'd both buckled up their seat belts. Ethan carefully laid the injured bird on the foldable table and prepped a bandage, while Sage pulled out a syringe and vial from the field kit for the meds. Neither of them spoke but he could read her face. She was determined to save this bird.

Everything she did lately, after what she'd told him on the beach, spoke volumes about why she'd chosen this profession. She was obviously haunted by losing her parents in that fire, and her dog too. What the hell must that have been like? Unimaginable. Her love of animals ran deep, her need to care for them and save them when no one else could. He would do everything he could to make her job easier, he realised as she raised the syringe and the chopper bumped around mid-air. And that involved not kissing her.

'Sorry, guys, the wind's getting up,' the mayor's voice echoed from the radio.

'Steady now,' Ethan murmured, holding the bird gently on both sides of its fragile body as Sage administered the medication slowly.

'I'm always careful,' she said through gritted teeth, taking the bandage from him and getting to work while he continued to steady the finch and ease some water into its dehydrated mouth. The medication had to be enough, but what if it wasn't? Its breathing was laboured, its eyes were closed, the poor thing could barely move.

His gaze lingered on Sage, the furrow of concentration between her brows. He itched to tell her that it would be OK, but it wouldn't be fair, so he didn't. In truth, the bird didn't look at all good now. Each breath from its fluffy chest seemed more difficult than the last, and the towel on the table was blood-soaked, its colour growing increasingly darker. The mayor was doing his best to avoid more bumps, but Ethan's instincts were on red alert; none of this was making much of a difference.

'That cat did a real number on him,' Sage cried. This time he didn't pretend he couldn't hear her. They were both watching the bird's chest rise and fall with less vigour, even as he held the oxygen to its beak. Sage's hands faltered slightly.

'Come on, little one,' he encouraged, hoping to be a mantra of hope against an encroaching shadow of inevitability. This bird's life was ebbing away between them. Sure enough, all too soon, the heartbeat beneath his fingertips stilled. Sage's shoulders slumped and her fists clenched.

'Damn it,' she muttered, not looking at him. Her voice was a heavy growl of anger and sorrow that tightened Ethan's throat. When he put a hand to her shoulder her green eyes brimmed with resignation and sent a chill up his arm—they'd failed. They hadn't even made it back to the clinic.

'I'm so sorry, Sage—'

'I suppose it was a long shot, considering the injuries,' she said, swiping her damp forehead. Any sparks he'd felt before felt smothered by the finality in her tone. He'd seen death before in a hundred innocent creatures, the end of suffering, the quiet exit from pain that was often as beautiful as it was distressing for those left behind, but somehow the loss of this rare bird felt personal, tied to the woman beside him and everything she had already lost. Sage turned to the mayor and told him what had happened. Ethan wrapped the delicate bird carefully in a clean towel, watching her body language. Her posture was telling him more than words ever could; she was definitely taking it personally.

'Hey,' he said. 'You did everything you possibly could.'

Her gaze flickered to him. For a second, Ethan thought he saw the walls she'd built around herself tremble, but she squared her shoulders and sniffed. 'Sometimes it's just not enough though, is it?'

The silence returned, heavy and oppressive as they descended over Amber Creek. When the helicopter touched down in the adjacent field and the blades wound down, Sage didn't even wait for the rotors to stop turning before she thanked the mayor and disembarked with the bird in the towel, her steps hurried as she made for the clinic.

Ethan made to jump out after her but the mayor was faster. 'Ethan. Make sure she's OK, yeah?'

He paused with the supplies, his gaze tracking her as she made for the gate to the property. He was about to ask the other man what he meant, but he decided it was pointless. You could tell a lot about Sage Dawson by how she walked or held her head, the things she wasn't saying. He'd picked up on that already but the mayor had known her longer. She was putting on a brave face now, but they could both tell she was shaken.

'She goes out of her way to do these things, and we all want to help her, knowing what she's been through, you know?' the mayor said, looking over his sunglasses at him, as if inviting him to reveal he knew exactly what she'd *been through*.

Again, Ethan almost asked how he was supposed to know what Sage had been through, but again, it would have been pointless. Sage was best friends with this man's wife—she'd probably told Abigail about their conversations…and their almost kiss… The mayor would likely know he'd been getting closer to Sage than to Storm since taking on this project.

'I'll keep an eye on her, make sure she's OK,' he reassured him.

'Good man, take her out or something, make her laugh. She needs it.'

Ethan nodded resolutely. 'Yes, sir,' he said, remembering this man was the one who'd hired him, and trusted him, and who'd *also* dropped everything to try and help save a rare bird. He would do it for the mayor as well as for Sage, he decided, because taking Sage out, feeling the way he was starting to feel about her, was the last thing he should be doing, really.

CHAPTER NINE

THE RHYTHMIC KNOCK on the flimsy wooden door of her cabin startled Sage from her reading. She glanced up at the clock—six minutes past eight. She moved the plate of half-eaten toast from the duvet, her heart racing as she folded the corner of the page in her book, and flicked the needle off her vintage record player. She wasn't expecting company.

'Hey, Sage? You OK in there?'

Ethan's deep voice carried through the thin barrier with an undercurrent of concern at the sudden absence of her jazz music, and she stood up too quickly. She'd seen him through the windows before settling down to read, his muscular silhouette moving around the paddock with Storm. He and Billy had finally managed to saddle him but she'd forced herself not to watch, to mind her own business. The day's events had taken their toll, another almost-kiss that had freaked her out, an unpreventable death, all of it confusing and sad and now she wanted to hide away from it on her own.

She opened the door to find him standing there. The moonlight cast long shadows across his angular features. His blue eyes searched her face.

Oh, Lord, why do you have to be so gorgeous, Ethan, and why did I tell you this wasn't a good idea...?

'What can I do for you, Ethan?' she said instead.

'It's been a tough day,' he confessed with a weary smile that melted some tiny frozen-over part of her. 'I could use a drink. What do you say we go out somewhere?'

Sage clutched her book to her chest. That look in his eyes was unnerving. The way he'd said *'You...'* earlier at the clinic, before they'd been interrupted by the call about the finch, had been playing on her mind. *'You...'* As though he'd been about to confess something she was doing to unnerve him. It had turned her inside out.

This chemistry between them was undeniable, and after their first almost-kiss it had started to affect her concentration—it was why she'd done her best to undo it all in the chopper. Why start something up that would just go wrong and leave her worse off than she was, thinking even *worse* things about herself? He'd pretended not to hear her.

'Actually, I was about to go see some friends.'

Sage stepped aside, inviting him in anyway. How could she not? The walls felt as if they'd closed in tighter with Ethan's broad shoulders moving past her in the confines of her small living quarters. His scent caught her nostrils, mixed with soft hay, and she tried not to groan.

'Some friends?' he asked now, with a small smirk. She rolled her eyes at him.

'Yes.' Did he think she didn't have many friends, except Abigail? He was right, though. She really needed to get out more.

'You can come too, if you like,' she said, trying to keep her tone even while her mind buzzed with questions. Why did she just invite him to the only place she ever went at night besides Abigail's? What did he think of her home? Too humble, too cluttered with all her veterinary journals and second-hand furniture? 'Sorry about the mess, by the way.'

'This isn't a mess,' he said, casting an eye over her record collection before perching on the corner of the tattered leather couch and picking up the book she'd just put down. 'You should've seen the chaos at Jacqueline's house last Christmas.'

'Jacqueline?'

'My sister,' he said, flicking absently through the pages. 'My niece and nephew, little terrors… Kara's six, Jayson's eight, they're like a tornado of toys. One day when I was there, they decided it was the perfect time to test out their theory that the ceiling fan could carry their weight and help them fly.'

Sage raised an eyebrow, her earlier tension giving way to a grin. 'And you stopped this... experiment?'

'Caught them red-handed, chairs stacked on tables, tinsel everywhere. I had to channel my inner negotiator to get them down.' His laughter was infectious, so rare from him, but clearly coming from a place of deep love and affection and, for a fleeting moment, Sage felt a lightness she hadn't known she'd needed. He had come here on a mission to make her smile, she realised. Because of the dead bird. Or maybe he just felt sorry for her, she thought suddenly, now she'd told him how her family died. Did he think she couldn't cope when things got tough? She frowned. Maybe she was overreacting... Ugh—too many confusing emotions, it was hard to know what to think around this guy, but she'd invited him out with her now, so she was stuck with the consequences, whatever those might be.

She crossed to the corner where her shoes lay scattered, her well-worn slippers now seeming embarrassingly inadequate. 'Just need to change out of these.'

'I've got a pair just like them,' Ethan told her, with a nod to her slippers. 'Comfiest things ever.'

Sage smiled, feeling another shard of ice thaw inside her at the thought of sharing something so trivial with this man. She couldn't really imagine someone so masculine and active sitting about the house wearing slippers, stopping kids from attaching themselves to ceiling fans. And she hadn't known he had a sister, and a niece and nephew. Seeing how comfortable he'd been with Abigail's children, she'd bet he was a great uncle to them.

Beneath this new warmth and appreciation, tension coiled tight in her belly. The proximity of him in the small room magnified every breath, every shift of movement. As she bent to slip on her boots, she felt him watching her, but, standing up, she caught his gaze lingering on an old photograph of her with her mum and dad. The pride in her parents' eyes was immortalised right there in the picture, all three of them standing by the swimming pool after she'd completed her one-hundred-metre race and come in first place. The medal around her neck was so huge it covered her stomach.

'I was nine,' she said, looking at the photo with him. Then she felt his eyes on her again. Did he see the way she ached so badly to turn back time? She waited for him to bring it up, to ask more questions about her parents, but he didn't.

'Ready?' He broke the silence that had stretched too thin between them and she opened the door for him to walk ahead.

'Sounds like you're quite the uncle,' she remarked as they stepped out into the balmy evening air. Somehow she hadn't pictured him with anyone else from his family besides his dad. He always seemed so solitary, as if all he did outside working with his horses was hang out even more with his horses.

'I love the little monsters,' he quipped, making her laugh. He was pretty good at dissolving tension when he wanted to, she thought, gratefully. Also pretty good at making her forget she should be staying away from him.

The sky above was a canvas of ink around the moon. It hung like a solitary lantern amongst the stars as Sage clutched the straps of her backpack. Thank goodness it was cool out now. They walked side by side along the dusty path that curled behind the clinic, and she tried not to think about the fact that his presence out here in the silence was already sending a stampede of horses to her chest in place of her heart.

The mayor had almost certainly put him up to this, told him to check on her, and stupidly she'd invited him further than her doorstep, where she probably should have just thanked him for his well wishes and closed the door. It was hard, though, to resist this softer side of him. To think she had once assumed he was more style than substance, only good for posing for the cameras! The more she got to know him, the more he proved he was actually a really decent guy and a great vet.

The crunch of gravel underfoot was the only sound now, and the rhythm seemed to pulse with unspoken words. She was already turning this into something it wasn't.

So silly! Just calm down, Sage.

She glanced at Ethan, his handsome, way too kissable profile etched against the night sky, and felt that familiar pull, the one that tied her stomach in knots. He was close enough that she could see the contours of his face soften in the moonlight, but he wouldn't try to kiss her again, she'd made sure of that. Surely she had done enough to keep him at arm's length, at least as far as a romance was concerned. He was only here now because of the mayor, anyway.

The possibility that he might not be interested in her after all caused her thoughts to spiral, her confusion mingling with the cool night air.

'So, where are we going?' Ethan's question sliced through her reverie.

'You'll see,' she told him, but her voice came out distant and distracted. She wrapped her arms around herself. Why had she invited him along? This was something she always did alone. Maybe she *did* want a fling…maybe she should just stop being a wuss and kiss him! But flings led to feelings and she knew her heart couldn't handle someone else she admired and cared for disappearing on her.

She stopped just short of the familiar tree, her eyes tracing the constellations in the sky above them as she slid the backpack from her shoulders. Ethan stifled a smile.

'I thought you were seeing friends?' he said, his voice low and curious.

'And here they are.' She didn't look at him as she pointed skyward. 'Up there,' she whispered, spreading out the soft pink blanket she always brought with her, and dropping to the ground. He was here now, so she might as well reveal her secret.

'That bright one, that's my mum, Caroline,' she said. 'And next to her, that's my dad, Anthony. The little one that sparkles a bit differently? That's Juni, my Australian Shepherd.'

Ethan lay beside her, his body a solid presence. His silence instantly comforted and unnerved her at the same time. He probably thought she was completely crazy. 'What do you talk to them about?' he asked instead and she felt the heave of relief lift her heart. Of course he wouldn't judge her; he knew what it was like to lose loved ones.

'Everything. You mean to say *you* don't talk to the stars yourself?'

He smirked, shook his head. 'No, but I might have to start. At least they don't talk back.'

'Neither do animals,' she reasoned.

'Which is exactly why we like them, stars and animals. Peaceful beings. Mostly unargumentative.'

'Exactly.'

She stole another glance at him, at the strong line of his jaw, the faint stubble that was growing on him, and her too. He was more than what people saw on TV. So much more than what she had expected to see, when he'd first shown up in his sexy jeans and boots with enough charisma to charm a nation. With her he was both open and closed, revealing these small parts of himself to her piece by piece, only to withdraw again, protecting himself.

A lot like she was doing, she realised now. He'd been through enough himself to warrant him being a little cautious when it came to their obvious chemistry. But he did feel it, with her—it was pretty much undeniable when the panic and confusion around her own feelings subsided. Should she kiss him now? It would be so easy.

No. Sage, what are you doing?

'So you come here all the time?' Ethan said.

'I do. Always alone,' she added.

He nodded. 'Well, thank you for introducing me to your family.'

His gaze followed hers as she stared at all the sparkling celestial bodies she'd assigned to her loved ones, and various other animals she'd lost over the years.

'What happened that day?' he ventured gently after a moment. 'The fire?'

Oh, man, here we go.

Sage drew a shuddering breath as her chest and every bone seemed to tighten inside her. 'I should've helped them…' Her voice trailed off, choked by the weight of it like always, heightened by the loss today. That poor bird.

If she said too much, he'd find an excuse to leave, he'd link her to the stories that had done the rounds when they were kids, that still resurfaced now sometimes, thanks to the Internet. Bryce had loved all animals, just like Ethan. Bryce had turned his back on her and Ethan would, too.

Ethan shifted, propping himself up on his elbow to look at her. He seemed to see the battle in her eyes and for a second the whole story formed on her tongue, but she willed herself to keep quiet.

'What do you mean, you should have *helped* them?'

She bit her tongue.

'Sage?'

She released a small sigh through her nostrils. 'I was looking at my phone, in the main house,' she said eventually. 'That night. We were camping out front—my dad loved us all to do that. Campfires, stories, hot dogs on the flames, no technology. I needed the bathroom in the house, so I went inside, and then of course I sneaked a look at my phone and got distracted chatting with my friends, and when I came back, the wind must have changed direction and…the fire was… everywhere. I hadn't noticed on my way into the house that our campfire was starting to spread outside the pit we'd dug.'

Ethan was still studying her closely. Sage's mind spun. Any moment now she would stop talking, if only her head weren't processing it all over again and sending it straight out of her mouth into his understanding, way too hypnotic eyes.

'They couldn't get past it. It just kept spreading,' she continued. 'My phone was back in the house. I *could* have just run back there but I didn't. I completely froze.'

'You were just a kid,' he said, putting a hand over hers softly.

She sighed. 'I wasn't a *stupid* kid, Ethan. I could have done something. Instead, my family died, and the fire spread out of control and all those poor animals in the bush… I can't ever forgive myself for any of it. If I hadn't been so selfish, and absorbed in my phone, if I just hadn't gone behind their backs to check it in the first place, I would have got there in time to—'

'Sage!' He sat up straighter now, reached for both her hands. She was looking at him through a blur of tears, as if it had all happened yesterday. Great, she was already way too emotional because of the bird's death. It had brought everything roaring back to the surface. 'What happened wasn't your fault,' he pressed. 'Please don't tell me you've been carrying this guilt around all this time. Fires spread, that's what fires *do*.'

Sage's throat tightened around her next words. She turned away, ashamed of the tidal wave building up in her chest, and the tears he was bringing out of her.

'Tell me, sweetheart,' he urged gently, stroking the backs of her hands with soft thumbs.

'Everyone says there was nothing I could have done,' she confessed, her breath hitching, 'but I failed them all, I know I did. I should have seen—'

'You didn't fail anyone,' Ethan insisted, his tone firm and compassionate all at once. 'You were only a little girl.' He squeezed her hands in reassurance and she watched his hands tightening around hers, big hands, safe hands. Did he even know how she had wanted someone to understand all this, to talk to someone other than Abigail about it?

'You're making a difference every day, Sage. That counts for something. I'm inspired by you. Look what you've done here, for the people and for the animals. And for yourself.'

Sage's fingers curled around his now, grounding her in the present, in Ethan. It was such a re-

lief, feeling as though someone truly saw her.
Then… 'Did you just call me *sweetheart*?'

The word cut through her suddenly. Bryce had
called her that once, before he'd changed his mind
about her and disappeared from her life completely.

Ethan was studying her mouth now in silence,
tracing the lines of her face with those all-see-
ing blue eyes again, and she swallowed, drawing
strength from him. He was still here, he wasn't
getting up to leave. 'The last person I told about
the animals couldn't handle it at all,' she said before she could think straight. 'It was a guy, actually.' She glanced up at him, checking for a
reaction, but he was unreadable. 'He broke things
off with me. Well, actually he didn't even do that.
He just disappeared without ever speaking to me
again.'

Ethan shook his head gravely, and gave her
hands a final reassuring clasp before rolling to
his back again. 'Well, maybe he had a different
reason for going,' he said, looking up towards
the southern cross while her heart continued to
pound at his closeness and everything she'd just
spilled out after telling herself she wouldn't. What
was it about Ethan that made her want to talk?
She was just like one of his horses already, responding from a place deep inside her that she
couldn't fathom.

Then he turned his head to her. 'Did this man

actually *say* he was breaking things off with you because some animals died in a fire that wasn't even your fault?'

Sage opened her mouth to talk, but nothing came out, so she closed it again.

'Who was he?' he demanded gently.

Sage swallowed, measuring the seriousness in his eyes. 'A Canadian man I was seeing, called Bryce.'

'And Bryce just *disappeared*, right after you told him about that night?'

She nodded slowly, cringing. 'It was the morning after,' she admitted. 'And nobody else knew why he left the koala reserve, because he didn't tell anyone he was leaving.'

Ethan was nodding to himself slowly, still looking at the sky. 'Which koala reserve was it?'

She told him, and his eyebrows drew together. 'I've heard about that place. It's notorious for not paying people who show up without work visas and still expect to be paid.'

Sage combed back through her memories. Come to think of it, Bryce had once said something about not getting the money he'd been promised for the work he'd done there. Being an Australian citizen herself, she had never had a problem getting paid, so she'd forgotten about it. Also, she'd had a lot going on at that point, namely opening herself up to a man for the first time since vet school. She'd been a recluse, pretty much, till Bryce, aside from a couple of brief flings that had gone nowhere. Her work had been far more important to her, and she'd let everyone know it.

Her mind reeled; she must have zoned out because when she came back to herself, Ethan had changed the subject already.

'Did you know that Alpha Centauri is actually three stars, not one? And it's the closest star system to our own,' Ethan said, nudging her out of her reverie. 'And over there, that's the Carina Nebula…'

'The Carina-Sagittarius Arm of the Milky Way galaxy, I know. Almost nine thousand light years from Earth. Can you imagine how long it would take to get there?'

'Or what we'd find?' he added. 'I see I'm not about to impress *you* with my star facts.'

'You can try?' She shrugged. Was she flirting now? How did they get here from what they'd just been talking about?

Sage's heart pumped furiously as they talked about the stars and veered onto the subject of the cosmos and the probability of aliens and the intricate connections that bound humans to each other and to the world. For a while she forgot about Bryce entirely—who cared why he'd left at this point, anyway? She was distracted by the fact that she could talk to Ethan about anything, she realised as they lay there on the ground, side by side. But then, she couldn't quite muster the courage to ask any more about what had happened with his ex-fiancée and his best friend, and he didn't bring it up. Had he had a relationship since Carrie, of any length? A fling, maybe? If she asked him now, would he think she was sizing him up as more than a colleague and friend? Were they even *friends* now?

They were barely touching but somehow they were still travelling the world together tonight. It had been so long since she'd had a conversation like this with a man. Being friends with Ethan would be OK. A friend like him was welcome. If only she didn't still want to rip his shirt off and get inside his bed as well as his head!

In no time at all two hours had passed and they were both fighting back their yawns mid conversation. Ethan walked her back to the front door, told her it had been a pleasure meeting her friends, and Sage waited a few seconds longer than she should have, gazing into his mesmerising eyes before realising he most definitely was not planning to kiss her this time. He seemed different, as if he'd drawn a line under the whole idea, and once again she cursed what she'd said to him in the chopper.

'Goodnight, Sage,' he reiterated.

I liked it when you called me sweetheart more, she wanted to say.

But she let him go.

She groaned to herself as she listened to his ute pulling away. Who was she kidding? She could never make Ethan her friend. She'd never wanted to be with *anybody* as much as this in her life, but she couldn't have him. He was going to disappear out of her life, just as Bryce had, eventually. And there was no way she was going through that again, whatever the reason.

CHAPTER TEN

THE UTE'S ENGINE ROARED, cutting a furious path through the dense bushland. Sage clung to the dashboard, her knuckles white as the vehicle lurched over another unseen dip in the rugged earth. Beside her, Ethan's hands were steady on the wheel, his jaw set with determination. 'How much further?' he asked her.

'Should just be over this ridge,' she said, squinting at the coordinates on her phone against the glare of the sun. It was doing its best to blaze through the canopy overhead.

'Are we sure it was caught in a trap?' Ethan asked, his voice mirroring the unrest inside her, not least because they'd left the clinic at the speed of light after a local hiker had sent coordinates to them, telling them a dingo was stuck. Sage replied, her gaze not leaving the rough track ahead.

'Yes. She said the poor thing didn't look too good, but she couldn't stay with it, because she was out of water herself, and then she had to search for a phone signal.' As she said it, she noticed the bars on her own phone were fading from five right down to one. 'It's all alone right now, the poor thing.'

'We'll find it,' Ethan assured her, pressing his foot to the gas again.

Sage tried to focus on the dusty path, hatching a plan to help free the dingo whatever state it might be in, but her thoughts kept drifting back to the other night, last week, the last time they'd sat alone talking, under the stars. He'd helped her at the weekend with the irrigation system as promised, stopping only to answer a call from his dad. They'd chatted as they'd worked, but only on the topic of sustainable gardening practices. Nothing deep. Nothing personal. It was killing her.

It was almost as though that whole night alone with him under the sky had been a dream, and he'd closed off again, deeming her too broken maybe, as Bryce probably had? Ethan had made her think for a moment that maybe there had been another reason why Bryce had disappeared on her, but she couldn't figure out what that might have been. Why hadn't he just talked to her about it before he'd left?

The stars had been the only witness to her and Ethan's conversation that night. Now, as they drove deeper into isolation, surrounded by the twisted trees and sprawling scrub, the memory of Ethan's hand in hers that night, how nice it had felt, how safe and reassuring, wove itself so stubbornly around her heart she knew she'd be able to recall it fifty years from now, even if they never saw each other again once Storm was healed. Was it wrong that she was starting to wish Storm would never recover fully, that Ethan would have to stay here for ever and start doing more than just holding her hand?

'Here!' Ethan braked hard. The ute skidded to a stop. As they stepped out into the dust, the silence of the bush greeted them both like a living entity. They found the dingo just beyond a thicket of mulga bushes.

'Oh, you sweet thing, look at you.' The creature's furry leg was firmly caught in the grip of a rusted steel trap. 'The farmers just don't know what they're doing when they set out to get kangaroos,' she told Ethan. The dog-like animal's eyes were wild with pain as it lay panting, its coat matted with dirt and blood.

'Don't get too close,' Ethan warned her as she got to her knees. 'He's scared.'

'I know,' she told him, approaching slowly while he grabbed the bag from the ute. She crouched over the wounded creature, murmuring soothingly, even as it snarled in self-defence. Its teeth were tiny razors and Ethan put a hand to her shoulder, warning her to let him try something. At first, she ignored him, determined to do things her way. It was still so frustrating that he was here, on her turf, working his methods with

more success than she was having with hers…
but when the dingo snapped at her again and she
narrowly missed a sharp bite she stood back in
resignation and let him take over. She watched
him lay his hands on the animal, how it immediately stilled beneath him.

'Easy there, mate,' he whispered, his voice
low and soothing as he slipped a muzzle over its
mouth as a precaution. The dingo had already
stopped trying to bite. Sage just swiped her hot
forehead and let him assess the damage to its hind
leg. Their closeness, with bare arms and knees
in their respective T-shirts and shorts, shot bolts
of awareness through her bloodstream, though
she tried to concentrate on the mission at hand.

That night, after she'd told him about Bryce…
after he'd got her thinking about what really might
have happened to make Bryce leave… Ethan had
walked her back to her door like a gentleman, and
left her to think about it some more. Only now,
the more she thought about why Bryce left, she
couldn't help but think that maybe he just hadn't
been that into her…not in the way she'd wanted
him to be, after trusting him with all her secrets.
Maybe she'd just been a brief holiday romance
for him, and she had turned it into something
more. He'd seen his chance to make a break for
it, and like a coward he'd taken it without even
talking to her first. For whatever reason, Bryce
was long gone, and now Ethan was here. For a

while at least. She could have invited him into her home. This time, if she got the chance, she would accept it for what it was, a fling, a bit of fun, and she wouldn't get attached.

I should have just invited him in...

'Pass the bolt cutters,' he requested. Sage did so without a word and he concentrated on the task with fierce intensity, his muscular forearms glistening with sweat. With gentle, precise movements, they worked in tandem to free the dingo and soon the nasty trap was cast aside. She tossed it into the back of the ute, where it couldn't harm anyone else, and felt Ethan's gaze on her as she carefully applied iodine to the animal's injured leg. She continued with her soothing words, although it had stopped trying to lunge for her too now, as if it knew they were trying to help. She was even able to apply dissolving stitches and an antibiotic shot and she knew that together they were giving it the best shot at survival they could.

Ethan's admiration for her—or for her work, at least—was evident even without words. It felt nice when he looked at her so approvingly and worked with her like this. It made her feel guilty for not wanting him here at first and for not trusting in his methods. His methods worked for him, and by proxy they were working for her too. Ethan knew that every creature was of equal importance to her: a dingo was no different from a rare, endangered bird. Losing either was another heartbreak, to her at least. He knew that now and he knew why she felt that way, because she'd told him everything. And now the air around them crackled with an electric charge as another shared mission brought them closer, beyond the physical.

Sage allowed herself a fleeting glance up at him, her pulse quickening as the sunlight played across the angles of his handsome face. He'd shone a new light on the whole Bryce thing, making her wonder if she should gain closure by looking him up and finally *asking* him what had happened. Ugh, why couldn't she just get over it? It was as if, as soon as she decided to try, the guilt crept back in and stopped her. Despite Ethan's reassurances, nothing would *ever* make her feel differently about the way she'd let her family down. How could she ever shake the guilt over what had happened? How would she continue to live if she lost anyone else she cared about? That was the biggest reason she hadn't initiated anything with *this* man.

Ethan told her to stand back and she obeyed, watching him unclasp the muzzle. The dingo limped away, and a rush of pride blocked everything out for a moment. She turned to him, and before she knew what she was doing she'd held her hand up ready for his. Their palms met in an awkward high-five that somehow morphed into something resembling a clasp.

'Nice job, boss,' Ethan said.

'I'm not really your boss,' Sage huffed, swigging from her canteen, trying to ignore the hum of awareness that zipped along her nerves as his thumbs brushed the back of her hand. 'You're on the mayor's payroll, remember.'

Ethan's eyes held hers, and she found herself lost in their vivid blue depths for a heartbeat too long, trapped as the dingo had been. She knew why he called her boss, really. Because it was better for him to see her like that, an illusion of safety.

'It suits you, being a boss lady,' he said, thoughtfully, motioning her back to the truck.

The drive back began in silence along a different route. Sage focused on the landscape unfurling outside the window—a tapestry of greens and browns all punctuated by the brilliant blue sky above. None of it was enough to distract her from the fact that Ethan knew everything about the night of the fire, which had formed the very backbone of her existence, yet she still knew next to nothing about him really; not when it came to matters of the heart. Maybe it was too soon after Carrie for him to feel right about initiating anything with her, someone who would soon be operating tasks like this alone, thousands of miles away from him. Torture. Maybe he really did still have feelings for his ex, despite how she'd betrayed him with his best friend?

The pull towards this man, who hadn't judged her in the slightest, was getting impossible to ignore.

'Watch out for the—' Sage's warning came about three seconds too late. A jolt threw her against her seat belt as the ute's front wheel caught on something. Ethan wrestled with the steering wheel, his jaw set in determination as he tried to manoeuvre out of whatever was ensnaring them, but it was no good. Each attempt only seemed to dig them deeper into the earth. He cursed under his breath, throwing the ute into reverse. It still wouldn't move.

'Here, let me try,' Sage said, unbuckling her seat belt. As she stepped from the vehicle with him the issue was immediately apparent. They were ensnared in a network of tree roots that would be a pretty impressive work of nature if it didn't mean their vehicle was totally stuck. They swapped places and she gripped the steering wheel with the familiar surge of adrenaline that came with a challenge. The engine growled as she tried to manoeuvre them out, but the roots held fast.

'Stubborn thing,' she muttered in frustration.

'Like someone else I know,' Ethan teased through the window, a half-smile softening his features.

'Ha-ha, I had to try,' Sage shot back, though secretly she appreciated the lightness in his voice.

It was rare to see this side of Ethan—the same one he'd revealed when he'd been talking about his sister and his niece and nephew that night under the stars and, later, all the speculation about aliens and the cosmos. It was impossible to think there was nothing else out there when you lived under skies like this. The thoughtful philosopher was yet another facet to him that wasn't at all like the larger than life, sometimes arrogant personality the TV had portrayed, but still, the revelation did nothing to free the trapped tyre.

'Looks like we're going to be stuck here for a bit,' he said, his gaze meeting hers.

'Seems so, yes.' The tension flew back in between them and wove itself through her frustration like a fine thread, till she stepped back out of the ute into the dust, shutting the door behind her with a sigh. Her thoughts were in a frenzy, trying to come up with a solution while also avoiding the intense energy that seemed to surround them as he approached. She nervously watched him move around the car opposite her as they circled it together, inspecting the tangled mess of roots once more. Sage fumbled for her phone, her heart sinking as she swiped the screen. No bars. Not even a flicker. She met Ethan's expectant eyes and shook her head. 'Still no signal,' she reported. The isolation enveloped them like a second skin.

'Maybe if we dig around the tyre?' Ethan suggested, and she shrugged. They might as well try.

Sage's hands were caked with red dust as she clawed at the earth, her fingers aching from the effort. Ethan was beside her, his body bent in exertion as he dug around the trapped tyre with a piece of sturdy wood. The sun bore down on her shoulders, relentless in its late-afternoon fury.

'Almost there,' Ethan grunted, his voice threaded with dogged resolution. 'Just a bit more leverage and we should be able to rock it out.'

Sage wasn't so sure, but she didn't like to say it. She watched him swipe at his brow with the back of his hand, leaving a smear of dirt in its wake, and continued digging. She knew she really shouldn't be looking at Ethan's muscles bunching under his sweat-dampened shirt at the same time; her mouth was already dry enough as it was. But who would be able to help it?

'Ready?' he called out as she finally positioned herself behind the wheel yet again.

'Ready,' she echoed, finding him in the mirror. He braced himself against the ute's frame and started to push, straining against the metal beast, willing it to break free. The vehicle groaned, a low, protesting sound, and soon it lurched, once, twice, and again before settling stubbornly back into its earthen prison. Ethan swore softly, kicking at the stubborn root that was holding the wheel captive. Checking her phone again, she felt dread settle in.

'Still nothing. We're completely cut off.'

A heavy silence settled over them. It felt compounded by the vast, lonely wilderness that stretched endlessly in every direction. It was just them—the bush, the fading light, and all their unfinished business hanging in the air like ripe fruit. The thought of spending the night out here in the open wild sent a shiver down her spine despite the heat.

'Someone will be along soon. If not, it could be worse,' Ethan noted, scanning their surroundings. 'At least we've got that one water canteen, and some supplies…'

'We have trail mix,' she said, and he pulled a face, making them both smile for a second.

'It'll be fine.' She sighed, clinging to the practicality of the moment. But the sun wouldn't be up for much longer, its descent already painting the sky orange and pink. Maybe *someone* would realise they weren't home yet, and be along soon?

Ethan's silhouette cut through the dwindling light as he stooped to pick up another branch. 'We don't *need* a fire, you know,' he called over his shoulder, but the growing heap of wood beside him belied his words. She wished she could be as enthusiastic and as useful as he was, but they'd been out here an hour and a half already with no hope of rescue and she was hot and exhausted.

'Are you going to keep the wildlife away with your bare hands, then?' she retorted, and he flexed a biceps at her playfully. It was meant as a joke, but instead it made her insides flutter. He had no idea what his strength and physique, on top of his talents—not to mention his *eyes*—could do to a woman.

'Seriously, I've seen your "no naked flames" signs,' he said, tossing a bunch more sticks onto the pile. 'And now I understand why.'

'I'm fine with it, really,' Sage said quickly, gathering a smaller, more manageable stack for herself. The scent of eucalyptus rose from the bark and mingled with the earthy fragrance of the cooling ground. 'We need to save our phone batteries,' she added, trying to ignore the thrum of her heart that had started along with his concern. They were pretty close to the bush. But Ethan was here, and she couldn't let her old fears control her for ever. More to the point, she couldn't act like a fool in front of him when it was her fault they were stuck out here anyway. There had been warnings on the radio and from locals about the tree-root system. It was because of the drought—the ground was just too dry. What with the dingo, and her head being full of Ethan, she'd clean forgotten.

Ethan located the cigarette lighter from the ute

and coaxed the first flickers of life from the dry wood. Sage forced her feet not to take three steps backwards, instead inching closer. He shot her a look, as if to ask if this was *really* OK with her, and she nodded her silent consent. Thank goodness he was with her, really. Being out here alone would have been terrifying, and there was no way she'd have lit a fire on her own.

They'd pulled bags and a couple of spare towels from the ute to sit on, and soon the last of the dusk had faded from above them and the flames were curling up into the sky, spitting at the stars. What would her parents think if they could see her now? she mused, feeling Ethan's eyes on her again. He was picking at the last of the trail mix, which was all they had to eat.

'I'd murder a bowl of pasta right now,' he said, scrunching up the empty packet.

'Are you a good cook?' she asked curiously. She had never seen him cook a thing in the clinic's small kitchen.

Ethan nodded slowly. 'I can heat things up in saucepans, put pizzas on a rack, boil water in the microwave… That's what you mean by cooking, right?' he teased.

They started to talk about their favourite foods and Sage realised she was imagining him in a silly apron with boobs or something on the front, in a cosy kitchen with sunshine streaming through the windows. She was there too in this imaginary kitchen, stirring something in a pan on the stove. He was coming up behind her, coiling his arms around her waist, nuzzling her neck…

She chastised herself silently. *Sage, you are being totally ridiculous.*

'Here, drink some of this water,' Ethan said, handing her the canteen.

'Thanks.' Her fingers brushed against his as she took it, and a timely, inappropriate jolt attacked her core. She took a sip, busying herself with arranging the towel underneath her, trying to focus on the practicalities of settling into a night out here in the bush, rather than the warmth that lingered from his touch, or how much she wanted to sleep pressed against him. They talked about their favourite restaurants, his in Brisbane, hers mostly in Perth, and she tried to ignore the ache to ask him anything too personal, even though she was dying to.

'The fire feels nice,' Sage murmured without thinking. Ethan just raised his eyebrows and smiled, resting back on his elbows. It had actually grown a little chilly now that the heat of the sun was completely gone. She hugged her knees, the silence around them deep and full of unvoiced thoughts the second they stopped talking. Ethan swigged careful rations of the water, muscles shifting under the fabric of his shirt, shadows playing on his cheekbones. Sage couldn't concentrate any more. She also really had to pee.

'I have to go…' she told him, making to stand up.

'Need me to come too?' he asked her, sitting up straight. She laughed and shook her head, looking around for the non-existent bathroom.

As if.

'I can manage, thanks.'

'Well, take your phone for the torch, at least.'

'OK.'

The second she left the heat of the fire, the vastness of the sky and the shadows closed in. Silently she wandered to the nearest line of trees and crouched down close to the earth. What a situation this was. People were probably wondering where they were by now, but it was highly likely that no one wanted to take the path they'd all been warned about in the dark.

Sage was just doing her business when something sleek caught the corner of her eye. She turned her head slowly, her heart rate quickening as she flashed the phone's light around.

Where are you? What are you? Oh, my God.

Suddenly, she was frozen in a crouch. Just a couple of metres away, coiled among the underbrush, was a huge snake. It was hard to see its length exactly, but its scales glistened under the faint moonlight, reflecting a dangerous mix of black and deep red. She knew this one—a red belly. Highly toxic.

Sage's breath caught in her throat. This was not ideal—she'd been mere steps away from this creature while she'd just relieved herself! The gravity of the situation sank in, right as the creature decided to move again. A scream instinctively clawed its way up her throat, but she bit it back, not wanting to alarm Ethan. She had to stay composed.

Calm, calm, calm...

Careful not to make any sudden movements that might provoke the snake, she rose slowly from her crouched position, her heart pounding against her chest like a trapped bird.

Calm, calm, calm...

Her mind raced as she weighed her options, right as Ethan appeared from behind the tree. She almost jumped out of her skin as she fumbled to do her buttons up, eyes darting from him to the snake. She couldn't see it any more, it had moved. 'Ethan...'

'Sorry, sorry,' he said, shielding his eyes. 'You were just gone too long and I was worried.' He went to move towards her but she held up her hands.

'Snake,' she hissed.

He froze on the spot, just as she had. 'Where?'

'It was just here!'

'I don't see it. You must have scared it off.'

Even so, he shone the torch around as a warning as he led them both back to their makeshift camp. The fire was blazing now, its crackle deafening in the hush of the evening. The flames leaped and twirled and she forced herself not to move further back, to embrace it. It was a good thing tonight, keeping all the bad things at bay. Ethan's features had hardened, the lines of strain around his eyes more pronounced as he sat closer to her than he had before, shoulder to shoulder, alert and aware, as if he'd assumed guard duty on the lookout for snakes on attack.

Sage had dealt with snakes her whole life, but she'd let him protect her, she decided. Ethan was quiet for a few moments, contemplating the fire. Then he turned to her and out of nowhere he asked: 'So, that guy Bryce. Was it serious between you two?'

CHAPTER ELEVEN

ETHAN WAITED FOR her reply, studying her lips close up in the firelight. Maybe he shouldn't have asked such a personal question but, after hearing everything about the fire that killed her family, he was still putting the pieces of the Sage puzzle together. She'd tortured herself over what had happened that night, completely unnecessarily he was sure, and that guilt had affected so much of her life. As it had with Bryce; the way she'd just assumed he'd left because of something she'd done or hadn't done as a child.

She chewed her lip, looked at him sideways. 'It was just a little fun, I suppose,' she told him warily, fidgeting on their makeshift blankets.

'How long did you have fun for?' He looked over her shoulder for the snake, before focusing on her eyes again.

'Why do you care?' she asked, digging a stick into the dirt between her feet.

He studied her brown boots, the way one of

the laces was coming undone, and nodded quietly. He'd asked for that.

'You're right, it's none of my business.'

She sighed. 'It was just a few months, and, looking back on it now, it was nothing serious. I mean, I'm like you, I guess. I don't really *do* relationships.'

'Is that right?' He couldn't help the smirk that crossed his mouth.

'I'm pretty good at self-sabotaging my own happiness, in case you hadn't noticed,' she said tartly, straightening her shoulders. 'I suppose I always just assume...'

'That you don't deserve anyone's love or attention,' he finished. 'Which isn't true, by the way. I've said it before and I'll say it again. What happened to your family was not your fault. I really hope you know that.'

She pursed her lips but didn't answer.

'You were just a child. Would you really still be blaming anyone else for something that happened when they were ten? You're thirty-five, right? I saw your driver's license.'

Sage's eyes widened, before her brow furrowed into a deep frown, and he had to wonder whether anyone actually ever reminded her of this, whether she even talked to anyone about it, besides Abigail. She looked as if she was going to argue with him for a second, but then she tossed her stick into the fire and deflected away from her family. 'I don't know if I was ever really in love with Bryce anyway. I don't think I've ever really been in love with anyone.'

He didn't ask why, even though her quick glance at him made him acutely aware she was attracted to him. Her survivor's guilt, and her fear of letting someone in, only to lose them as she'd lost her parents, had dictated her whole life…the same way losing his mum, Cam and Carrie had dictated his. This was all dangerous ground, but here they were, and he wasn't just going to sit here in this weird silence.

'The more I think about it, I know I haven't,' she followed. 'I've certainly never wanted to marry anyone.' Sage's voice caught as her fingers twisted the edge of the towel. Ethan stared into the flames. Her hesitance to continue plunged them into another heavy silence.

'I proposed to Carrie because things hadn't been that great between us for a while,' he admitted after a moment. Sage pulled a face, and he grimaced. 'I know, I know. I just thought maybe it would keep us together—we always said we'd do it one day. It was the longest engagement anyway. Four years…'

'Four years?' Sage looked incredulous.

'We got engaged three years in, but we could never agree on a wedding date,' he explained, realising how silly it sounded now, even to his own ears. 'Looking back, I guess neither of our hearts had been in it for a long time. Carrie even stopped wearing the ring. It started when she lost interest in my life, in my horses and my family, everything I loved, you know? Everything she used to love about me…or said she did. Then I lost Mum and had to care for Dad and I guess it all just got too much for her. I was blindsided… or just blind, I suppose. I let my grief take over everything for a while, and I didn't even see her slipping away till she was gone.'

Sage listened closely, not interrupting. It felt strangely therapeutic to talk about it, even with her. 'How did you find out about the affair with Cam?' she asked.

Ethan scowled into the flames. He was saying things he'd never said to anyone but Jacqueline, but then, keeping it all stacked up inside him was toxic and he loathed small talk more than anything. Their crumbling communication had been the death of him and Carrie.

'I booked a hotel on the beach for Cam's birthday,' he said eventually. He explained how it was something they always did for each other on their birthdays, a guys' night away somewhere. Fishing, motorcycling, surfing, all that stuff. That year Carrie had really wanted to come, and he frowned to himself as he recounted it all, remembering how much Cam had advocated for her being there that year. 'We had dinner booked for seven, but a cat was knocked down by a car outside. I went to see if I could help. By the time I got back from the local vet I'd missed dinner. I heard Cam and Carrie talking in the suite…'

'They went to a suite together?'

'I'd booked the suite for Carrie and myself,' he said, explaining how he'd thought it was a little strange that they'd gone there instead of staying in the restaurant, or the bar. 'I was about to walk in but then I heard what they were saying.'

Sage touched his arm gently, her expression gently inquiring.

'It doesn't matter,' he said, his voice a low rumble. It really didn't matter; besides, there was no way he was telling her the exact conversation he'd overheard about his 'weird horsey stuff', and about how Carrie had dragged the wedding plans on because she didn't have the heart to break things off after his mum had died. How he'd then heard them kissing, convinced they were doing great at keeping their secret. 'I heard all the proof I needed that I was about to be given the boot, one way or another,' he said instead.

'What did you do?'

'Nothing, for a while.' He poked at the smouldering logs with a stick. 'I took myself down to the beach to clear my head. That's where Cam found me,' he said. 'I had it out with him, but Cam went on the defensive, telling me I hadn't been paying enough attention to Carrie, how she'd come to *him* and he'd fallen in love with her, and he hadn't been able to control it. I went and faced Carrie next,' he continued. 'She was angry...but more angry that I'd found out, I guess. Then she said she just didn't love me any more. That she'd tried to, but I wasn't the same person any more. Simple.'

'Seven years together—that doesn't sound simple.' Sage looked furious on his behalf all of a sudden, and while his own burning anger had turned to a mild, albeit perpetual simmer months ago her solidarity made her all the more attractive, all the more deserving of the truth that had driven him away from wanting another relationship.

'You lost your mother; how could you be the same person after that?'

'I'm fine,' he said quickly, even as the humiliation tore through him like a lightning bolt. It was true, he'd retreated, but Carrie hadn't been there for him either. 'It wouldn't have lasted anyway, me doing what I do, her doing what she does.'

He told her about Carrie being an actress, travelling city to city, party to rehearsal to late nights on the town with different casts and crews. His head and his heart had always been at the homestead, and now he was working towards making his mum's dreams a reality and making sure his dad never felt alone.

'You were just doing what you love, what you were born to do,' she reasoned kindly, and he ran his eyes over her lips, wondering why he was saying all this to her, while he could barely imagine Carrie's face any more.

'They're not like us,' he said. You're not a city girl, Sage, no more than I'm a city guy.'

'That is true.' She sighed. 'Cities have way too many people in them.'

'And you can't always see your friends when all those other lights are blinding you.'

'My friends?'

He pointed up at the sky and she smiled. 'Oh.'

The silence had shifted now into something comforting. 'I'd be lying if I said I didn't like it remote and quiet. Even though, tonight, I would have planned more of a dinner if I'd known we'd be out here *this* long.'

Sage was still smiling to herself. 'Sounds like a date, Ethan.'

Their eyes met and he knew they both felt this unspoken acknowledgment of the bond between them growing stronger, and tighter. It was a kind of quiet understanding he hadn't felt with anyone human in a long time. Only the horses.

'She'll never know what she's missing, you know,' Sage said next. Her tone was laced with so much sympathy and longing it drew the flames from their fire into his blood. He'd been cleansing himself of the pain of what Carrie and Cam had done to him just by talking about it with Sage and now he couldn't stand it any longer.

Ethan reached out, his hand brushing hers tentatively. She turned her palm upward, allowing their fingers to entwine as they'd done before, and his body responded in the exact same way, as though her touch was grounding any swirling emotions, pulling all his focus back to one place—her. He leaned closer, slowly, checking if she'd push him away.

The kiss was soft at first, exploratory, but it soon deepened as they both gave in. His heart thundered in his ears as he drank in the sweet taste of her mouth, and he let out a low moan that was swallowed up by the crackling of the fire. She felt so good in his arms. Sage's heart was racing against his chest as she pressed closer, her knees in the dirt as she straddled his lap, hips to his. Moving the way she was now… It turned him on so much he could hardly think. Their tongues danced together, teasing each other's mouths eagerly.

'Sage,' he heard himself groan, before she silenced him with another kiss. Her hands travelled up his chest and wrapped around his neck, holding him tightly as she deepened the kiss even more. Her breath was warm and ragged against his skin when she pulled away slightly.

'You taste like trail mix.' She smiled against his lips before sliding her tongue back into his mouth again. Their bodies swayed together with every passing second. He was lost in her now, they were lost in each other, and the rough bark digging into his backside as she writhed on top of him only seemed to add to the intensity of it all. It was almost as if nature itself were encouraging them onward and he groaned again with anticipation.

He lay back on the ground and brought her with him; they were wrapped up in each other, still kissing furiously. Every touch, every taste of Sage consumed him. The warmth of her breath against his skin, the sound of the crickets, the heat of the flames and the sensual urgency of her touch all made his blood rush around his body. He couldn't actually remember an encounter that could match this one. This woman was made from something different. He'd sensed it the first day they'd met. So what if this was a bad idea? It didn't have to be serious or complicated…just a fling. She didn't do relationships either—wasn't that what she'd said before?

'Ethan,' she moaned against his mouth, clearing his head again of everything but her.

Just enjoy this, he told himself, allowing his fingers to travel softly down around the curve of her waist, circling her navel. It was so hot when she shivered underneath him.

Sage's body was on fire. Ethan's tongue claimed her mouth over and over, dancing with hers as though he was trying to bury every thought that might be advising him against this, as though she was already his. His big, strong hands stroked her skin, sending shivers of butterflies round her belly and down her spine despite the fire. She gasped his name, pressing her eyes shut, losing herself again in the sweet sensations so her brain wouldn't get the better of her.

Stop worrying too much, she told herself. *Focus on the now a bit more, the things about this that are so good.* Right now, she felt more alive than she ever had.

'Ethan…' Her voice came as a breath against his mouth.

Just enjoy this, be in the moment, feel him… his fingers on your waist, curling around your hair, so soft, so gentle… God, I am shivering…

They'd rolled over and her back against the roughness of the ground felt deliciously wicked. The blankets and towels they'd set out were some-where else entirely now, they'd pushed them away, and the root system dug into her flesh as if it wanted to keep her there too, with their ve-hicle. He lay on top of her, propped up on his el-bows, arching into her, letting her move them both together.

Every tiny touch and caress and kiss drove her deeper into him. *So* connected, even without him inside her. This connection was everything, she thought to herself as her skin warmed at the fric-tion, at his kisses.

'Do you want this?' Ethan whispered against her neck, his breath hot against her skin.

Yes, yes, yes, never stop, she said in her head, but any vocal response was lost the second his lips were on her throat, kissing softly, sensually up the column of her neck.

The trembling started again, from her toes this time, right up through her core. His kisses grew more focused, more passionate, harder against her mouth, harder and harder, and harder.

His thighs around her waist pinned her, till she felt herself biting back a laugh at the sheer absurdity of herself like this, being here with him, pinned between these legs, deep diving into his soul, feeling with a non-refutable certainty that he wanted her despite what he knew she'd done. His fingers traced the line of her shoulder blades, following the gentle curve to the small of her back, then back up again.

His hands on my body feel so good. I love the way this feels when he's pinning me down.

Her eyes raked his muscled chest as he lifted his arms and slid off his shirt, tossing it aside to refocus all his attention on her, arching beneath him, locked between his rock-hard thighs, like a trapped animal. She sat up beneath him, letting his hands slide down her body, catching her breath as he slowly unbuttoned her blouse while trailing more soft kisses along her exposed skin. She had never felt this way before, completely and utterly surrendered to the kind of desire that was consuming them both in this moment.

He pulled away then, his gaze still burning with intensity as he looked down at her, his eyes searching hers for any sign of hesitation or uncertainty.

I want this, she confirmed with her eyes, and her hands, and another urgent kiss that felt as if it were binding his soul to hers.

Seemingly satisfied with her silent consent, Ethan trailed his fingers down to the waistband of her shorts, and he inched it down slowly, savouring every bit of skin that was revealed with another stroke of his thumb, or a groan that made her feel like more of a woman than she'd felt since…since when? It was actually hard to remember. Sage moaned into his mouth as he moved back between her thighs. She tangled her fingers in his hair and arched against him, wanting even more, all of him.

How is this happening?

His eyes were dark, full of desire and longing, making her start to perspire in places she hadn't been too aware of for a while. The firmness of him against her thigh was insistent, and huge.

Oh, my.

She could feel every inch of him now, with only their underwear between them, and the trembling, the anticipation, was too much to take.

She made to reach a hand into his boxer shorts, preparing herself.

Ethan stopped suddenly. Pure torment took over his face as he groaned in dismay and pulled away, sitting up on the ground beside her. Her heart lurched at her ribs as if a truck had slammed on the brakes a millisecond before hitting her.

'What's wrong?' she asked him breathlessly, sitting up beside him, suddenly self-conscious. She was more exposed than she'd ever been, and not just physically—her brain had just been somewhere else, dancing in a whole other universe, and they hadn't even had sex yet! If that was foreplay with Ethan, what the heck would the real thing be like?

Ethan looked at her with regret, making her insides swirl with dismay. 'We shouldn't do this, not right now,' he said with a growl.

'What?' Sage was confused, more than a little disappointed, and also… *What the heck?* 'Why not?'

Ethan shook his head. 'We don't have any protection,' he told her, tying back his hair that had come loose in their fit of passion.

'I have a coil,' she explained tightly, suddenly feeling silly. It was true, it helped calm her ridiculously heavy periods, but she hadn't expected to have to spell it out; she wouldn't be initiating sex if she wasn't protected against pregnancy, would she? Especially out here. He must know that.

'I'm sorry, I don't know what I was thinking. It's not you, OK? I just, I got carried away in the moment, but it's not fair to you.'

Sage nodded again. Not fair? This felt an awful lot like rejection. In fact right now she didn't trust herself to even speak. Her soul could not retract that fast, even if his could. Maybe sensing her disappointment and confusion, he took her hand again and kissed her palm gently. 'It doesn't mean I don't want you, trust me,' he followed, tracing a finger across her cheek in a way that made her breath catch.

OK...so he seems like he's telling the truth.

'I want you, Sage, more than you know.'

That same tortured expression came over his face again, and her heartbeat felt like a thousand kicking kangaroos all over her body.

But?

He was wrestling with emotions he was not going to talk about. Was it too soon for him after Carrie? After seven years of being with the same woman? How could she not think that, after everything he'd just told her? But she wouldn't mention her name, not after everything they'd just done.

Ethan shook his head at himself, and she couldn't help it, she reached for him again and kissed him, and for a moment, as he responded, all traces of uncertainty disappeared as she

melted into him again. All right, so they didn't
have to have sex right now, it was probably smart
not to, what with there being a snake and God
only knew what else on the loose that might bite
them…but when they were home again, somewhere safe, she was not going to allow any excuses. They'd started so they'd finish. Seriously,
it had been so long since she'd felt this good, there
was no way she'd deny herself an extension of
this…so to speak.

Sage pulled back and turned over on the
ground. Ethan draped a protective arm around
her body, pulling one of the giant towels over
them both. It felt like a shield against the night,
and everything else she'd been carrying around
that had been keeping her in this bubble of self-
defence and denial. Why on earth had she been
denying her own needs, her right as a woman to
feel this way, even if it was only for a little while?

She had to remember what he'd been through
with Carrie though, she thought, watching a
shooting star scurry across the sky so fast she
didn't even have time to mention it to him. It was
hard to believe he'd just shared all those awful
memories with her, and that he was here, holding
her close, leaving her in no doubt that he wanted
her. Maybe there was a side of Ethan only *she*
had been able to coax back out into the open.
Imagine that.

The thought made her smile as she snuggled into him as his little spoon. The warmth of his body curled around hers, his heart beating steadily against her back, the scent of the outdoors mingling with the lingering, delicious scent of his own personal sweat... This was enough for now. They lay there, wrapped up together, as Ethan's hand moved gently over her hair, his fingers trailing along her scalp in a soothing touch.

Ah, that feels so wonderful... I wish this night would last for ever.

'Sage, wake up!'

Ethan's voice broke into her dreams. Sage blinked her eyes open to the light of dawn creeping through the trees behind him. He'd already started scrambling for his clothes and she caught a brief glimpse of his impressive muscles before he yanked his jeans back on over his boxers. The sound of an engine hit her ears. How long had she been asleep?

'Oh, no!'

'Hurry,' he urged her, half laughing as he threw her shorts at her. The engine had been distant at first, but now it was growing steadily louder. Sage buttoned her top up wrong, and then hurriedly rebuttoned it, scanning the horizon.

'I think rescue is on its way,' he said, folding the towels up haphazardly and then much more carefully scattering the remains of their fire across the dirt. He'd left his shirt open and now she was fully awake, looking at the flexing of his six-pack in the early morning sunshine, all she wanted was to kiss him again.

CHAPTER TWELVE

THE UTE EMERGED over the ridge, and she recognised it instantly. 'Abigail!' Her friend's dusty old truck had seen more of the bush than most locals combined; she and the mayor knew these roads and everything off-grid around them for miles. The sight of her best friend coming for them should have brought unadulterated relief, she thought as Abigail and the mayor pulled to a stop and got out, but as Ethan shook the hand of the mayor, who quickly assessed the situation and started pulling tools out, Sage's emotions were a train wreck. She drew a deep breath, then another and another, closing her eyes, trying to find her equilibrium.

Abigail took her aside, her deep blue sundress swishing around her ankles, her giant sunglasses hiding her expressive eyes.

'Did you do this on purpose to get him alone out here?' her friend asked with a wicked smile.

'Of course I didn't,' she replied, a little too haughtily, watching Ethan sliding under the stuck ute with the bolt cutter. She rolled her eyes at herself, turning her back to him and facing Abigail head-on so her eyes wouldn't be forced to linger on Ethan's sexy body.

'I think I'm in big trouble,' she admitted with a sigh.

Abigail pushed her shoulder playfully. 'Have you gone and done the unthinkable, Miss Dawson?'

Sage cringed at the ground. 'Not quite. Almost.'

Abigail just grinned. 'I don't blame you,' she swooned. 'I mean, have you ever seen such a stunning specimen of a man?' Her gaze followed Ethan as he expertly manoeuvred the cutter around the tree's roots. 'I love my husband, but, really, possessing those arms and abs should be a criminal offence.'

Sage merely nodded. What could she say? Her head was still full of the warmth of his touch, the comforting rhythm of his heartbeat, everything they'd shared in the quiet darkness. Her heart ached at the thought of losing that connection with him so soon after she'd discovered it. Sage couldn't help the pang of loss overriding her thrill at having spent the night in his arms. Sex or no sex. The intimacy of it, all that shared vulnerability. It had felt so right, and so real. But now it seemed as though it was slipping away from her already. He'd said something like it wasn't fair to her. It wasn't fair of him to sleep with her? That had to mean he still had feelings for Carrie, didn't it?

'You're beating yourself up over this, I can tell,' Abigail observed quietly.

'He didn't want to, you know, he didn't want to have full sex with me,' she muttered, creasing her nose.

'Sage, look at where you are!' Abigail gestured around them as a tumbleweed floated past. 'It probably wasn't the time or the place. Maybe he's got some stuff going round in that big old handsome head of his, too. Am I right?'

She was pretty spot-on there, actually. 'Don't say anything, Abigail, keep it quiet, OK?' Before Abigail had a chance to say anything more, a holler from the guys told them the mission had been a success. The adventure was over; finally she could get home, and take a shower...with or without Ethan in it with her. Already she was flushed just thinking about what might happen next.

Sage and Ethan unloaded the gear from the back of the ute, while Abigail hurried inside to the bathroom and the mayor padded over to the stables to see Storm. 'I'm hoping I can saddle him up again, show the mayor how much better he's doing,' Ethan said as his hand brushed hers over the empty water canteen. The move sent a trail

of sparks right up her arm and she gripped the
canteen, its cool metal a stark contrast to the
scorching morning sun. Or was she hotter because of Ethan, and last night? She took a deep
breath, resting for a moment against the back of
the truck.

'Everything OK?' Ethan's ocean-deep eyes
searched her face. The intensity in them left
her feeling more exposed than she had last
night. She'd had to do a quick check in the ute
to make sure she hadn't buttoned anything else
up wrong—not that Abigail didn't know exactly
what had gone on. Why had she told her what
had happened…or what had almost happened?
Now the mayor would know, and there were no
secrets in Amber Creek, ever. The last thing she
wanted was for poor Ethan to think everyone was
talking about them.

'Of course I'm OK,' she said anyway, tuck-
ing a stray curl behind her ear. The memories
of what they'd shared last night were clinging
to her harder than the dust on her boots and he
was throwing her thoughts off track the more he
looked at her.

Ethan took the canteen from her hands gently, his gaze not leaving hers. 'You've been quiet
since we left. If I crossed a line—'

'I wanted us both to cross a line, Ethan. I
thought I made that perfectly clear.' The words
were out before she could stop them. Again. She

watched his eyes widen in amusement a second before they narrowed in speculation.

Oh, great, so now he thinks you're desperate for sex, Sage. How attractive, well done.

Ethan scratched at his chin. 'I'm sorry if I made things weird,' he said finally. 'I guess I got lost in my head after everything we were talking about and seeing you so...'

'So what?'

He growled to himself, low in his throat, and shook his head and she willed her hands not to reach out and touch him. 'I did think that maybe you're just not ready for that level of intimacy with someone else after—I mean, you were with her for years until pretty recently. And that's OK,' she lied.

'It's definitely not that,' he confirmed, and the incredulous look on his face made her cringe inwardly.

'Then, what is it?'

'You're making me kind of nervous here, Sage.'

Her heart lunged right for her throat again. She swung her head around. No one was watching or listening. Ethan's eyes were fixed on hers. 'You do the same to me,' she confided.

He sniffed, glanced sideways. 'The things I told you, I've never told anyone other than my sister.'

'Well, that makes two of us, only in my case it was Abigail,' she said.

Oh, Lord... Sage swallowed against the tightening of her throat as it threatened to choke her. He just kept looking at her as if he were scanning her brain, his jaw moving side to side as if he were chewing on his next words. Was the fact that she made him nervous a good thing, or a bad thing?

When he spoke, his voice was laced with a kind of knowing that sent shivers along her arms and between her thighs. 'I don't think we had a choice anyway, back there. What happened between us was always going to happen.'

Gosh, it was hot already. Sage reached for the bundle of towels to stop her hands from touching him again. The fabric unfurled slightly in her grasp. In an instant, the smile fell from her face. 'Yeow! What was that?'

Snatching her hand away, she sprang back from the ute, clutching her arm against her chest.

'What happened?' Ethan asked, his eyes flooded with concern.

'Something sharp, I don't know...' Her wrist was turning red already and the markings sent her blood cold. Two tiny punctuations, set close together. Then she saw it; a flicker of black and red slithering out from the folds of the towel she'd just dropped to the ground.

'Snake!' she cried out, stumbling backwards again. Her heart pounded against her ribs as if it wanted to run even further, but she sank to her knees in shock. 'It got me.'

Oh, no...no, no, no! This isn't happening.

Ethan leapt over the snake as it writhed on the ground as though it wasn't sure what was going on either, and he was at her side in a heartbeat, his hands examining her wrist with urgency. 'We need to get you into the clinic—now.'

Too late. A flash of pain seared her arm. The red-bellied black snake's poison was already doing its job, working its way into her system. Soon it would paralyse her. She watched, horrified as the creature slithered away and vanished into the brush. Shock morphed into ice-cold fear as reality sank in. It was the same snake that had watched her pee last night; it must have sneaked past their warm fire and up into the stationary ute while they were sleeping. And now it had sunk its fangs into her.

'Can you walk?' Ethan asked, his brows knitted with concern.

'Y-yes,' Sage stammered, fighting the dizziness that was threatening to consume her already. Could she? She wasn't sure. They had to move fast. The world was already swaying around her.

Seeing her rapid deterioration, Ethan scooped her up into his arms as if she weighed no more than a new-born foal and stepped up the pace. Cradled against his chest, she felt herself shrinking as somewhere in her periphery she saw the mayor sprinting towards them. Everything was moving in slow motion. Sage gritted her teeth against the pain, willing herself to stay conscious.

Do not pass out, Sage, do not pass out.

'Stay with me, Sage,' Ethan urged as if he could read her mind, and she held onto his voice like an anchor, fighting for something to make sense in the chaos of her thoughts.

That stupid snake...what did it want with me? Why did it do this? Oh...everything's so floaty...

'Sage, you're fine,' he stated with a confidence she couldn't quite believe. She was clutched tightly against his chest for all the wrong reasons, and a part of her mind that felt as though it existed outside herself replayed the warmth of him last night, as she'd snuggled into the protective circle of his arms.

It would be worth it, if she died like this, she thought groggily; at least she would go knowing nights like that could happen to her. And he'd just admitted he still wanted her...that he'd been processing everything, how nervous she made him feel because...because why? Had he actually given her a reason?

They burst through the door of the clinic. Abigail was on the way out from the bathroom. The mayor was right behind them now and somewhere she heard Ellie, back from sick leave, hurrying a customer out with their animal patient. She vaguely heard Ethan barking out orders, his years of experience evident even to her, in her state, in the way he took charge.

'Antivenom, now!' he commanded, sweeping whatever was on the long metal table to the floor with one hand and laying her down gently. It was hard to force herself to focus on him, but he squeezed her hand and she clung to him like a lifeline, her body trembling with shock and pain. Searing pain. It was snaking from her arm to her lungs, and her blood, it was on fire. How was this happening? One moment everything had been fine, and the next, she was here on her own cold, hard operating table, fighting for her life.

'Ethan,' Sage said hoarsely as her eyes focused in and out on the vial of antivenom he now had in his hand. Abigail clutched her other hand, while the mayor hovered behind on his phone. Who was he talking to? Their childminder?

It doesn't matter, Sage. Am I really dying?

'You're gonna be OK, my darling, just hold on.'

Ethan took her arm, which she couldn't even really feel at this point. He injected the serum and Sage winced, waiting for another sharp sting that never came. From somewhere that might have even been from outside herself again she saw Abigail's eyes flash to Ethan, then back to her, and she had the distinct impression one of them had just said something she'd do well to remember. But she was woozy…so woozy…

He mumbled something and soon she was fluttering in and out of a dreamy sleep. Moments later, or maybe it was an hour, it was hard to tell, she could feel the effects of the antidote taking hold. The world around her began to sharpen into focus again, and she realised with a start that Ethan was still holding her hand, his piercing narrowed eyes searching her face for any sign of distress.

Gosh, you're so handsome.

'Is she going to be all right?' Abigail's voice was laced with genuine worry beside her.

'I won't let anything happen to her,' Ethan replied with a conviction that made Sage's heart thud erratically all over again. It wasn't just the snake venom causing her pulse to race now. What was it she should be remembering? She tried to sit up on the table, causing a makeshift pillow under her head to fall to the floor. This was so embarrassing.

'Easy, Sage,' Ethan ordered, supporting her weight suddenly and urging her back down with an arm that felt like an iron band around her waist. Her senses slowly righted themselves, and she felt the warmth of his breath against her temple, real and intimate.

'Thank you,' she whispered into his eyes. Her voice was barely above a whisper. Her head was light, a residual venom-induced haze clouding her perception. But even through the fog, the expression on her best friend's face was clear as day. Abigail and Ellie had both seen Ethan's unguarded emotions out on show, his raw concern totally stripped of any professional facade. And so had she.

'We should get her to her cabin,' Ellie said just as Mrs Dalloway, one of their regular clients, walked in with a cat basket.

'I'll take her,' Abigail and Ethan said at the same time. Then Abigail relented, placed a soft hand to her cheek. 'Fine, you're stronger than me, Ethan. You can carry her.'

Embarrassment flooded her veins like a new serum. 'Thank you, Ethan, really, but...' She paused in her efforts to get up again, swallowing hard against a tidal wave of nausea. 'You need to be out there, helping with Storm. I'll be fine.'

'I'll see to Storm later.' His eyes were brimming with an emotion she couldn't quite name. Concern, yes—but there was something more now, something deeper.

'If you're sure,' she said with a feeble smile.

Ellie ushered a bewildered Mrs Dalloway and her cat through to the other room, insisting *she* would help with the patients and that the mayor could come back tomorrow. The short journey to Sage's quarters behind the clinic was a blur. All Sage could register was the rhythm of Ethan's movements and the sound of his voice reassuring her.

'Here we go, this is better than last night's cold,

hard ground,' he said as he located her bedroom, and gently laid her down on her bed. The cool pale-blue walls and bedsheets were a small comfort against the heat that was radiating from her skin. She still hadn't showered. This was a nightmare… Was her bedroom tidy? Had she put her laundry away or were her clean knickers still in a pile on the armchair? Was any of this suitable for a guest to see? It wasn't exactly how she had envisioned bringing Ethan here, or why.

'Please, Ethan, the others…' Sage began, her voice trailing off as another wave of dizziness hit her.

'All right,' Ethan conceded, though his blue eyes darkened with worry. 'I'll check back in with you really soon.' He put her phone down on the dresser. 'Call if you need anything.'

'Will do,' she managed to say, though the words felt like stones in her mouth. Maybe the snake bite had been fate stepping in, telling her not to get ahead of herself, not to sleep with him the moment he was ready, not to make whatever this was between them into something that would destroy her once it ended and he went home.

Ethan stood up, hesitating for a moment as if torn between duty and desire. He looked as if he was about to say something, but decided not to. Then, with one final, lingering look from the doorway, he left, closing the door quietly behind him.

Alone now, Sage closed her eyes, trying to

steady her breathing. Then she opened them and checked her chair for the laundry pile. Small blessings, she had at least put her knickers away. But Ethan's big, steady presence in her humble, small home still lingered like a tangible thing, wrapping around her in the quiet.

Now that the drama was over, she had had time to consider other things. *Ethan.* What was blossoming between them was real, wasn't it? Everyone had seen it now. He hadn't said it in so many words, except for when he'd called her darling… yes, that was it, that was what she'd forgotten! He'd called her darling, in front of everyone. Not Doctor, not even just Sage. *My darling.* Did that mean Ethan truly cared about her? She already cared about him, and that was even scarier than the thought of that snake, still out there somewhere, lying in wait for its next target.

CHAPTER THIRTEEN

ETHAN'S FINGERS TRACED the coarse hair of Storm's mane. The animal was standing calm and collected beneath his touch in the early hours and he'd watched the dawn break like this, the air cool and the paddock quiet, save for the occasional snort from the horses. His eyes locked with Storm's, a silent conversation flowing between them. Trust was not given freely in this world, he mused, especially not by an animal with a past shadowed by mistreatment like he suspected this one had dealt with. The more he worked with Storm, the more he figured the guy the mayor had bought him from had not been completely honest about his history. But Ethan sensed another definite breakthrough. They'd been coming more frequently. He and Billy had even managed to saddle him the other day, though Storm hadn't liked that much and had taken off around the paddock pretty quickly afterwards, snorting angry little snorts from his nostrils while the other horses looked on in amusement.

Ethan's eyes moved over Storm's back to Sage's quarters, just visible beyond the tree line. Her small cabin wasn't much but she'd made it her home and he'd been to visit her over the last few days, while she'd been resting. He'd forbidden her to work, as had Ellie, and as such he'd taken on more responsibilities around the place. The grass had even been mown, the irrigation system was well under way, and a new surprise would be arriving soon that he was pretty excited to share with her. He didn't mind the work, but the way he cared about it all with ever-increasing depth and passion was starting to unsettle him. He was doing it for Sage. It was all for her, and that indicated that he was starting to like her more than even he thought he did. But he had been down this road before and it scared the living daylights out of him.

'We can't help our feelings, though, can we, boy?' he said to Storm, who grunted indifferently, making him smile. He wanted that woman so badly. He'd wanted her that night out in the bush, but seeing her so vulnerable, after letting himself be so vulnerable in front of her, had pushed a barrage of what ifs into his brain that no amount of kissing or burying himself inside her would ever diminish. She was making him extremely nervous, and that was the truth. Terrified, in fact. This was a dangerous road to go down, but he couldn't deny that he wanted to, even more now.

'Morning,' a voice called out, pulling Ethan from his constant thoughts about Sage. She was walking towards him in the flesh, her footing steady but cautious. The vibrant green of her eyes seemed muted in the early morning light. It was a testament both to the ordeal she'd been through with that damn snake bite, dulling her light in general and keeping her laid up for the last few days, and to how he made her feel, which was clearly equally nervous. They wanted each other. And they were going to have each other.

And then he was going to miss her for a very, very long time, because, even if she came to Queensland for a visit and loved it, this was her home. After everything she'd lost, she'd bravely built a new life here with her practice and her small staff, the local community, and her found family—Abigail, the mayor and their children— and she wouldn't want to give it up any more than Carrie had wanted to give up her life for him. Grasping for a future with Sage would probably end the same way as *that* had, with him feeling less than what she really wanted or needed, and her chasing after something better.

'Hey,' he replied, watching her come closer. 'How are you feeling?'

'Better, thanks.' She stopped at the fence, leaning against it. 'I've been going stir-crazy in that bedroom.'

'Can't keep a good vet down, huh?' He smiled,

but he could hear the undercurrent of concern in his own voice, even as he fought the sudden uncharacteristic urge to make an ungentlemanly quip about what he could do to make her bedroom more exciting.

Not the time, not the place.

Sage's snake-bite incident had been drifting into his mind unasked-for ever since; the way her body had gone limp in his arms, her face ashen, the terror that had gripped his heart like an iron vice. Just seeing her like that had been hell. Pure torture. He was surprised his mind hadn't gone completely blank, that he'd managed to somehow stay calm and administer the antivenom, but in that crystallised moment he'd understood the depth of his feelings for her. The revelation was still churning around in his mind, as worrying as it was exhilarating.

'Those flowers you brought me, they're beautiful, Ethan. And the vinyl records…' She trailed off, her gaze flicking back to him. 'I didn't realise you knew I liked vintage jazz.'

'Your record collection gave you away,' he confessed, feeling his cheeks colour just slightly as he caught the hint of a smile on her lips. 'I figured you could use some company, even if it was just more Coltrane and Fitzgerald.'

'Just some of the most influential voices of their era,' she replied. 'Very thoughtful.' Her voice came out slightly strained, her eyes narrowed at the floor for a beat, as though she was struggling with the meaning of his gifts, as he was, he supposed. He'd gone to the tiny cafe in town, which doubled as a record shop, and the guy in there had known Sage, of course; he'd shown him what she didn't already have in her collection.

Ethan's hands stilled on Storm's mane, the weight of his thoughts growing heavy as hay-bales on his shoulders. He hadn't kissed her since their rescue from the dingo adventure. The urge had almost overwhelmed him, especially when he'd come by with the gifts, rearranged her pillows, made her tea.

They'd been pretty safe while she'd recovered. Her weakness and vulnerability had been every excuse not to lean in and pick up where they'd left off, but they were still perilously close to the edge. Whatever was growing between him and Sage was something that would not just go away, he knew it, as certain about that as he was about the trust growing in Storm's eyes. Even as he warned himself not to pursue it.

'Thank you, for everything you've done around here too. It means a lot to all of us,' Sage said now, breaking the quiet tension.

Longing and reminiscence tormented his senses as he nodded and pulled his eyes from her legs in those jean shorts—legs he remembered wrapped around him on a night that was probably best left forgotten. She was so near now, he could hear the soft rustle of her shirt against her skin as she moved. How could he forget how her shirt had come off that night, how she'd revealed herself so willingly? Sage was beautiful, inside and out. He cleared his throat.

'Any time,' he replied, before turning to study Storm's eyes. The horse's ears flicked back suddenly as Sage inched closer. The ghosts of this horse's old fears were still there. He could totally relate, he thought ruefully.

'You can tell, can't you?' Sage asked, stepping backwards again, her voice low and steady beside him. 'You know what's wrong with him.'

'Every time I touch him. It's like he's decided to let me in,' Ethan said, his fingers tracing a faint line along the horse's flank as he met her eyes. They were standing close enough to feel the warmth of each other's bodies without touching, and he willed himself not to move even closer or he'd have to give in and make love to her right here. 'He's been traumatised by humans. It's in the way he flinches at sudden movements, how his eyes constantly dart around searching for an escape.'

Ethan caught a glimpse of pride on her face as she looked at him, which was not how she'd looked at him before, when she'd clearly been wishing he'd never shown up at all. She ran a hand over Storm's soft neck. 'Is there anything we can do to help him recover fully?' Her question held hope, but the shadows beneath her green eyes told Ethan she understood their limitations. 'Or will he always be like this?'

'Time and patience,' he murmured. 'He's getting better. Trust doesn't come easy, not when it's obviously been shattered before.'

'Like with some people we know,' Sage agreed, and Ethan felt her words like a gentle accusation. He knew she was talking about him. Or maybe both of them?

'Sage, listen—' he started, stepping around the horse. But the moment was interrupted by a call from his dad. Oh, man. Dad had the kids and Jacqueline over. He quickly explained to Sage how Kara and Jayson were collecting honey and probably wanted to show him on a video call, and she nodded encouragingly, though he didn't miss the flash of despondency in her eyes as he spoke to his family, *oohing* and *aahing* over their finds, pretending he'd never seen any of it before, to amuse the kids. No sooner had he hung up than the sharp ring of the clinic's emergency bell sounded out. Without another word, both of them broke into a run.

Ellie was still caught up with their first patient in the treatment room, and Ethan recognised the kindly Barbara from the guest house, or Babs as everyone in Amber Creek called her, standing over her terrier. The dog lay whimpering on the examination table. His paw was swollen, and a thin line of blood seeped worryingly through his fur as Sage hurried to pull a white coat over her shirt and shorts.

'Marley jumped off the porch again,' Babs explained as Ethan pulled on his own coat. The woman who had been so kind to him at the guest house was wringing her hands, her usually warm face etched with worry.

'Let's check for fractures,' Sage directed. Her professional demeanour had kicked in again, full throttle. She went for the X-ray machine as Ethan moved to calm Babs.

'Marley's strong, Babs. We're going to take good care of him,' Ethan assured her, his hand firm on her shoulder. He didn't miss the look on Sage's face as she looked up; was that an expression of slight despondency on her face, the same as he'd seen outside? No time to think about it now.

Ethan helped Sage manoeuvre the terrier onto the radiography table. The machine hummed to life, casting a pale blue light over Marley's form as they positioned him gently. Ethan watched the rhythmic rise and fall of Sage's chest as she leaned over the operating table, her focus unwavering. The marks on her wrist were uncovered, healing well just as she was, but the sight of them only reminded him of how it had felt when she'd been lying so weak in his arms. She operated the controls while Ethan held the dog still, his hands firm yet comforting against the terrier's quivering body. So small and defenceless...as Sage had been that night, when he'd rushed her into the clinic after the snake had got its fangs into her.

'Good boy, Marley,' Sage whispered now, eyeing the animal as the X-ray did its silent work. Sage couldn't stand to see any animal in pain, especially dogs. It was like this for her every time, he imagined. And it would be after he was back home with Dad, and the bees, and his own horses.

The image soon appeared on the screen, revealing a minor fracture. Sage discussed the treatment plan with Babs, explaining the need for a cast and pain management. Ethan prepared the syringe with expert precision, his movements conveying the quiet confidence he knew would help ease Babs' distress.

'Will he be okay to walk on it?' Babs asked, her voice concerned.

'Absolutely,' he answered, before Sage narrowed her eyes slightly and continued before he could.

'But he'll have to take it easy for a few weeks. No more jumping up, or chasing sheep.'

As Sage applied the cast, Ethan observed the gentle way her fingers smoothed the edges, and how she spoke softly to Marley, reassuring the animal with every touch. Even so, she was annoyed about something now. It was plain to him, even if Babs wasn't picking up on it. Was she starting to resent him again, for befriending all her clients? he wondered suddenly. Amber Creek was so small, of course he'd got to know a lot of people here, and he'd showcased methods that had worked as well as hers, if not better sometimes. It didn't mean he was trying to take over.

'Thank you, both of you,' Babs said, relief flooding her features as she finally scooped Marley into her arms, the newly applied cast a stark white against his ruffled brown fur.

'Any time, Babs,' Ethan said, offering her a smile that he hoped had reached his eyes. When she left with Marley cradled close against her chest, he turned to find Sage watching him, a set of unspoken grievances lingering between them.

'You called her Babs,' she said, perching on the edge of the desk, pulling off her gloves slowly finger by finger.

'That's what everyone calls her,' he reasoned. What was the problem?

'Well, Babs loves you. Everyone knows you round here now,' she said. 'They all know you're leaving again soon, though. Once Storm is better. Which he is…he's almost better.'

He felt his eyebrows knit together. 'So *that's* what this is about,' he said sharply. 'Me leaving.'

'Well, you will be, won't you?' she said, standing up and tossing her gloves into the bin a little too hard. He heard her voice crack. The tension hummed between them like a charged circuit. 'Storm is like a different animal already.'

She crossed to the sink and turned the tap on full, as if she was trying to drown out the noise in her head. Ethan watched as the water cascaded over Sage's hands, the droplets splashing against the stainless steel. He knew she was struggling, her emotions churning beneath the surface as his had been for days. He stepped forward, the linoleum floor creaking quietly beneath his boots. With each step, he felt his heart beat louder in his chest, till he was right behind her. He reached out and turned off the tap, silencing the rushing water.

'Sage,' he said gently. Slowly she turned in his arms and looked up at him. Her green eyes held a mix of vulnerability and sadness that tore at his heart. Without hesitating, he closed the distance left between them and gently cupped her face in his hands. To his surprise she turned her head away, even though her lips trembled at his touch.

'No. This has to stop,' she said, her voice weak and shaky. She drew a hand across her mouth, as if she was intent on stopping him from even so much as looking at her lips.

'We didn't do anything,' he replied, feeling the weight of his unvoiced confession heavy on his tongue. God, he wanted her so badly, even if it was only one time. One delicious, thrilling, beautiful time. The guilt over these exact thoughts didn't sit well—she would never go for a one-time thing, and nor should she be expected to. But he had stopped what they'd started before this. And yes, he had then gone on to buy her gifts, sat at her side, folded her clean towels, ordered her a new coffee machine...which still had not arrived. No wonder she was as confused as he was.

'Yes, we *did* do something,' she said, running her fingers over her lips, meeting his eyes. 'It's not just about sex to me, Ethan. You've made me feel things I haven't felt before...for anyone.'

She screwed up her nose then, and stepped out from between his arms, moving to the other side of the room. 'You bought me books, and flowers...'

'OK, well, sorry?' This was confusing as hell. And ridiculous. He needed to confront this, whatever 'this' was between them. He couldn't leave with regrets, with what ifs haunting him across the miles.

'I don't know what's going on either,' he admitted, crossing to her again. She inched against the closed door, pressing her back to it, and he placed his hand gently on her arm, feeling the warmth of her skin beneath his fingertips, even through her lab coat.

'You know what you do to me—you've seen it. But I don't want to hurt you,' he said.

Which was true, even though the voice in his

head was screaming, *Liar! It's you who doesn't want to get hurt.*

'I'm not staying here. I can't—my life is in Queensland,' he heard himself say anyway. Maybe it *was* too soon after Carrie to trust someone else with his heart.

'And mine is here,' she said sadly, so close to his mouth he could feel the heat of her breath on his lips. 'So I guess that's that. It goes no further, Ethan.'

He studied her mouth in silence. Stuff that. It had nothing to do with Carrie being the last woman he'd been intimate with. It had everything to do with falling for Sage, plunging him straight back into a deep, dark funk that he'd only just climbed out of. *Coward.* Fear should not, and would not, dictate his choices any more.

Ethan closed the remaining distance between them, this time with an urgency that made her gasp as he finally captured her pink lips with his own. Their breathing grew heavier as they lost themselves. Moving one hand to his neck, Sage trailed it down to his chest as their tongues danced, no doubt feeling the pounding of his heart beneath his skin. Tugging her coat undone with one swipe, he pressed his body against hers, pinning her to the door with a new urgency that sprang from nowhere.

Sage folded against him in surrender, moaning softly into his mouth. Her breath hitched with anticipation and he leaned into the kiss, cupping her backside, squeezing it gently, then possessively. Her kisses and lips rained over his face, exploring every inch, and his hands roamed to her thighs, pushing them further apart as he grasped at her shorts, pulling them gently but firmly down to allow him access...

A knock on the door behind them made him shudder. Sage sprang out from under him, pulled up her shorts, and started buttoning up her coat. 'Coming!' she called, sounding delightfully flustered.

He felt himself grin. 'Really? I wasn't even close,' he whispered. She pretended to slap him, casting her eyes to the bulge in his jeans. He caught her hand and pressed his mouth to hers again hard, and she laughed under his kisses before letting her tongue dance seductively around his once more.

'I have to go,' she whispered frantically, pressing both palms flat to his chest. 'You should get back outside to Storm. The mayor will be here again soon.'

She made to open the door, first smoothing down strands of her hair that had fallen from her ponytail in their passion.

'Hey, Sage,' Ethan called after her, his heart hammering against his ribs with the adrenaline. Sage turned, a question in her green eyes as she touched a finger to her lips. There was no stopping this thing now, judging by the hope that flickered in her gaze, and the way he heard his own voice soften whenever he spoke her name. He was gone. A lost cause.

'Come riding with me, this evening,' he said. 'There's a place I found the other day I want to show you.'

He watched her expression shift through surprise, joy, and something akin to fear, before she took a deep breath. 'Sure, Ethan,' she answered, her smile finally reaching her eyes. 'Why not?'

CHAPTER FOURTEEN

THEY GALLOPED IN SILENCE, apart from the thundering hooves that broke the stillness of the night, sending up mini dust clouds that threw Ethan into a sandy blur ahead of her. Sage couldn't help grinning as the world was reduced to the wind's rush in her ears, and the magnetic pull of this incredible man riding beside her. She tightened her grip around the reins as her horse picked up speed, racing alongside Ethan on Karma.

The pale glow of the moon bathed the land around them in a silver sheen, turning the rugged landscape into an ethereal dreamscape that felt all the more surreal because she knew, at the end of this, that she would be making love to Ethan, if they still had the energy after last night. They'd shut themselves into her cabin, listening to the rain again, and he'd reached for her, pulling her closer as the jazz filled the air in her tiny living room, his hands moving with the gentleness of someone who was treating a wild animal with care. His touch still made her shiver, sending goosebumps spreading across her skin. She could feel the desire for him coursing through her veins every time, as if she could never get enough.

Night-time rides had become their unspoken ritual for the past couple of weeks, even in the recent rains. It could have been something to do with being out with him in particular, but Sage felt that the wild pulse of the land had started to call her: *Don't work so hard, get out of your head, come and be happy!*

The way he looked at her, the softening of those guarded blue eyes, told her she had helped take a battering ram to some of the walls he'd built around himself, and he had definitely brought something else out in her.

The part of her that had always been so captivated by nature and these beautiful, rugged landscapes had been shaken fully awake. There were new reasons to breathe now, more space in her tired lungs to sync with her surroundings, and Ethan Matthews. Less time to tie herself to the past, and fewer reasons to feel trapped in the cage she'd locked herself into all this time. In Ethan's arms she was discovering parts of herself she hadn't even known existed.

'Where are we going?' she called to him now.

'You'll see. If you can keep up.'

Sometimes she could feel her heart swelling, as though it were learning how to adjust to being so full after so long. She caught another glimpse of Ethan's profile, determined as they started to race. When the moonlight hit him just right she could have sworn he was from another planet. Oh, Lord, this was completely crazy. This big, huge, all-consuming feeling for him had sprouted from a tiny seed of reluctant admiration into something she couldn't even define. There weren't enough words to express how she felt.

'Too slow!' he teased her now, kicking his heels to Karma and speeding on ahead, even faster towards the horizon, daring her to follow. Their first ride, he'd taken her to a waterfall she'd known about for a while, but she'd pretended she'd never seen it before. He'd known she was pretending, of course. So the next night, she'd shown him a special place she'd known he wouldn't have seen: a circle of earth-red rocks still boasting aboriginal art in red and black markings. After each escapade they would have sex…a lot of sex, everywhere, anywhere. It had started out as just sex anyway. The last couple of nights had definitely felt more as if they were making love.

The word felt so strange, even as it grew in her own head. Love. It was more like a kaleidoscope, constantly changing colours and patterns in her mind, leading her thoughts down different paths she hadn't dared to travel in a long time. It was overwhelming, but the world seemed different now, as if with Ethan at her side in work, and pleasure—a lot of pleasure—she was seeing everything through a different lens. Colours were heightened and vivid, details were clearer, her patients seemed to smile more around her because she was smiling more at them, and everything was tinged with a sense of wonder and magic.

With Ethan, she felt truly seen, and not just for the compassionate veterinarian she had come to be known as in Amber Creek's small community. He made her feel as if she could do anything. This profound connection they seemed to share had almost stitched the fragmented pieces of her heart back together. If only she could summon the courage to tell him she wanted him to stay.

If she said that, she might ruin it all, she thought now with a stab of fear, watching his broad shoulders as he took the lead again, the way the trees seemed to bend in the wind to welcome him. She would probably hear, 'I can't stay,' or, 'Don't talk about that now, let's just enjoy the moment,' and those words would cement the end of the spell for good. Obviously, this was too perfect to last. She knew he'd have to go back to Queensland. It was just something she was trying not to think about right now.

The fear of people disappearing without notice from her life had kept her life pretty small. Yes, she'd been successful with her career, but life had to be about more than making money; what was it for if you couldn't share any of it? She'd blocked out her need for companionship, stubbed it out like a cigarette by keeping herself busy, but the loneliness and emptiness had a habit of sneaking up on her anyway. Her empty home had echoed with it, till now. Now her humble cabin at the back of the clinic was filled with laughter and all the secrets she and Ethan shared in the dark.

Because of it, and because of him, she had even found the courage to reach out to Bryce. Wouldn't it be good to get some closure after all this time, confirmation that Ethan was right—that he'd left so suddenly because of some discrepancy or altercation over outstanding pay, or purely just because he wasn't into her, instead of because he'd taken offence over all those animals that had perished because she hadn't put the fire out in time?

'Woah!' Ethan's deep booming voice broke through her thoughts. They'd ridden to where the sands met the rainforest, but she couldn't quite figure out where they were exactly. Good thing she trusted Ethan, although since the last time they'd found themselves stuck somewhere for the night she had been careful to bring a spare two-way radio, just in case.

'We're here,' he announced as the horses slowed without another word from either of them. Sage realised her heart was pounding from more than just the exhilarating ride. In awe, she drank in the sight before her. The relatively hidden glade seemed to pulse with an alien glow under the moon. A ribbon of water reflected its beams, creating a desert oasis that felt as though it had been created just for them.

'I've never seen this place,' she said in wonder, following him forwards on her horse. It was as if they'd stumbled upon a secret that had somehow been kept for centuries.

'Welcome to Star Creek,' Ethan announced, his voice brimming with pride as he slid off Karma with ease. 'I found it when I was tracking that herd of wild horses the other day.'

Sage dismounted, her legs shaky not just from the ride but also from the pure beauty of the place. How was it possible she had never seen this before?

'I've never even heard of Star Creek,' she confessed as they both moved to tie up their horses, giving them a rest and a chance to drink from the creek. He looped his arms around her and pulled her close, dropping a soft kiss to her forehead that still sent sparks flying from her head down to her feet.

'That's because I named it myself. I think the recent rains must have helped it form,' he said. And she kissed him again because she could, and because, of course, this hot wizard had managed to find something out here in the nothingness that she'd never seen before. Together, they explored along the bank of the creek, their footsteps quiet on the soft earth. The air was alive with the sound of crickets and cicadas, and other nocturnal creatures. The serenade to the night was a living pulse, and her heartbeat matched its thrum as Ethan's hand found hers, their fingers intertwining naturally.

They settled near the edge of the oasis and Ethan pulled a bottle from his saddlebag. It was wine, he told her, aged and apparently special, saved for a moment such as this. 'Where did you get it?' she asked.

'Babs brought it over, to thank us for looking after her dog. You were with another patient so I thought I'd surprise you somewhere special.'

It felt as though she was the only woman in the entire world he'd ever looked at like this. Then he leaned down and drew her into a kiss that made her insides fill with balloons that threatened to float her up into the sky. He uncorked the bottle with a flourish and whipped out two glasses that he'd carefully wrapped in towels, handing her one so she could take the first sip. The wine was rich and full bodied, and as the taste of it filled her mouth, she let her head rest softly on his shoulder, looking up at the stars. This was perfection. Having him here with her was perfection. Maybe she should risk it and ask him about his plans after this—ask him to stay longer? Or would that seem too needy? Maybe she should just relax and leave it to fate and the stars, and see what unfolded naturally?

'Look at that,' he said, pointing upwards, and

she smiled as she caught the particularly bright star he meant, twinkling above them. 'That one seems new to me, what do you think?'

'It could be a UFO,' she teased.

He smirked. 'Take me to your leader.'

'Let's name it anyway,' Sage said, caught up in the moment. There were lots of them like this, filled with a kind of childlike excitement that Abigail declared was disgusting, even though she said it with the utmost affection. They suggested different names for the star as Ethan's fingers trailed softly along the back of her neck in slow movements that made her shiver with desire. They kissed for a long time before refocusing on the star.

'I want to call it Hope,' she said after a while.

'Hope,' Ethan echoed, his thumb brushing over her knuckles. 'I like that.'

'It used to be a pretty alien feeling to me,' she added with a sigh. There was no way she was going to tell him, but she really *hoped* he wouldn't decide he'd had enough of her company once Storm was fully recovered. She was filled with so much hope she was bursting with it some days, but somehow she couldn't bring herself to put him on the spot and ask him what this was exactly. What *were* they? It felt like more than just a fling, more real than anything she'd ever experienced in her whole life. It was unprecedented and had sprung up from nowhere and now that it was here, she couldn't imagine living without it. No one had ever made her feel like this, as if she could face anything.

With the taste of the wine lingering on her lips, she felt the confession bubbling inside her. It was no good, she couldn't keep it from him. 'I reached out to Bryce the other day,' she said finally, her words coming out slowly as she gathered up the courage.

'Bryce?' Ethan's hand stiffened around hers. Suddenly his expression turned impenetrable.

'I felt I needed to know why he really left the sanctuary, why he left…me. To give me some closure.' She watched him carefully, searching for any sign of understanding in his deep blue eyes.

Ethan released her hand and looped his arms around his knees, picking up his wine glass again and twirling the liquid in it around. 'And did he reply?' he asked neutrally, his voice level but distant. He was acting as though he'd retreated behind a wall all of a sudden.

'Not yet,' she admitted, a twinge of regret making her shuffle her boots. Did he think she was a bit silly for doing this, for reaching back into the past like this, looking for an affirmation that probably wouldn't even come? The silence stretched between them, her unspoken thoughts turning into heavy weights.

'Closure is important,' he said quietly, though

his eyes didn't meet hers. 'Unless you want him back, of course.'

What? Sage snorted in indignation. 'Why would I want him back? That was just a fling. It was nothing like what we have…'

Ethan tightened his lips.

Oh, no. Why did I say that?

She heard him release a deep breath through his nose as he studied the water, as if he couldn't risk meeting her eyes now. The words had just fallen out of her, she'd blurted them at him before she'd even had a chance to rein them in. Great, now she'd gone and admitted how obsessed she was with him, that she thought being with him was more than a fling, when he'd never mentioned it being anything at all.

'Do you need him to remind you that what happened to your family and the bushland around your home wasn't your fault, or are you ever going to start believing that for yourself?' he cut in quickly.

What? Sage's heart dropped into her boots. Why was he changing the subject away from him, and them?

'Because I've been telling you that for weeks,' he continued, 'and I'm sure Abigail has reminded you of it too. I would hope that, even if I'm not here, you'll at least remember that, Sage.'

Even if I'm not here… OK, then. Now she knew.
She chewed on her lip, rocking on the spot

as she hugged her knees. The words sounded so final, like a message he'd been waiting to clarify at the first chance he got. The silence grew louder and louder, until it rang in her ears and made her head hurt.

'I don't know what I want Bryce to say,' she said finally, realising it was true. She'd found the confidence to reach out, but she supposed it really didn't matter what Bryce said or did in response. His opinions of her had ceased to matter a long time ago. It was herself she'd always had issues with; her crippling fear of people entering her life and then leaving her again with nothing but ashes.

Ethan drank his wine quietly, and she wanted so badly to ask him what was on his mind, to ask if this was a fling or if it *could* possibly be more, if they both found the courage. But no... the mood was totally ruined now. He looked as if a storm was going on between his temples. Like Bryce, he *was* going to leave her. It was probably what he'd been thinking ever since they'd started whatever this was: that they'd just have sex and keep each other warm at night until he finished the job with Storm.

He'd never deceived her; he didn't do relationships. He'd told her that himself. He also had to go home; he'd warned her about that, too. He had a successful, thriving equine centre on prime, lush land, a million memories of his mother, and a father who still counted on him. She'd been so wrapped up in him, she'd conveniently forgotten all that…or more like chosen to ignore it.

Don't say anything, you'll just make it worse, she warned herself.

Instead, she took another sip of wine, letting the flavours distract her momentarily from the questions that had started to claw at the edges of her new-found confidence. This was going to end badly, so it would probably do her good to back off a bit, before it really was too late.

CHAPTER FIFTEEN

ETHAN STOOD, ARMS CROSSED, in the shadow-dappled stables, the sound of hooves stamping softly against the hay-covered ground blending with the distant hum of the bush. Mornings were quiet, peaceful. He was starting to enjoy them too, especially the part where he woke up with Sage in her bed. He watched her now, unboxing the delivery. It was finally here; it had taken ages to arrive. Mind you, he thought, everything did out here.

'Ethan, what did you do?' Her brow furrowed in puzzlement that quickly melted into surprise as she pulled off the last of the brown paper and got down to the giant square box.

'Is this…?' She trailed off, pulling the sleek new coffee machine from its cardboard confines, gasping in surprise.

'Don't drop it,' he said, swiping it from her quickly, biting back a smile. He loved nothing more than seeing this woman happy, even though he should probably get used to not seeing her smile, and not hearing her laugh, and not waking up next to her hair tickling his face on the pillow next to him.

'Figured we could use a decent shot of caffeine around here that we didn't have to kick something to get,' he managed, his own voice sounding gruff with attempted nonchalance.

'You're the best.' Sage's green eyes met his, and he caught them with his gaze. He knew her eyes by now, in every kind of light. He knew when she was genuinely happy, like now, and when she was retreating, holding something back, as she had been for the past few days, since he'd taken her to Star Creek.

'Thank you, Ethan. This means more than you know. The rest of the staff will be so thrilled!'

I did it for you, he wanted to say, but he didn't because she already knew. Well, she *should* know. Things had been a little weird recently, though, and if he was honest, her gratitude, simple and sincere, was perforating the tension that had been hanging between them like a heavy curtain.

They'd been close in the most physical of ways over the past weeks, their bodies moving and talking without words, and that had started to make him feel infallible. But even as their mouths and hands and limbs found their way under the sheets, or in the hay right here—clichéd as it was—he knew it would soon be his last night here, and the longer he tried to delay the inevitable, the more painful saying goodbye would be.

He couldn't move out here, he was too embedded in his homeland, in his business and his family, and why would any feelings she might have for him override her need to be where *she* belonged? He was not enough. As he hadn't been for Carrie.

'I thought you'd like it,' he said, stuffing his hands in his pockets to keep from reaching out to her. 'It's a good one, right?'

'Definitely a good one,' she agreed with a smile that didn't quite reach her eyes.

She turned to examine the machine, and Ethan's gaze lingered on the wavy chestnut hair falling like a sleek horse's tail down her back. There were so many questions now. They'd been coming at him for days like barbed hooks waiting to tear open the worst of his wounds.

Maybe she would find someone else soon— possibly even Bryce, if she listened to his explanation for leaving, understood it and forgave him. She'd have every right to, seeing as he himself didn't do relationships. This was the rock and the hard place.

He just didn't know if he could ever trust another woman with his heart. Carrie had been so thrilled when he'd slipped the ring on her finger, as if nothing could ever be more important than them or their relationship and their plans, and look how *that* turned out. Carrie could be bare-

BECKY WICKS   195

foot and pregnant with Cam's baby by now, for all he knew.

The past kept clinging to him like a ten-tonne koala, strangling any ounce of courage he mustered when it came to really talking to Sage about what came after this. Dad and Jacqueline had both said he should ask her to come and visit Queensland, to try it out, to see if she might like it there. But his walls had shot back up that night at Star Creek, brick by emotional brick, and he still hadn't really let them down. The second she'd clammed up on him, he'd done the same. What he wanted, what he needed, really, was to not get in any deeper.

Damn it, man, you're always overthinking things. Just ask her to visit Queensland!

'Hey,' he heard himself say, the word slicing through the silence. 'So, I've been thinking...'

'About?' Sage prompted.

'Queensland.' The word felt like a stone in his mouth, heavy and hard.

She flinched. 'Ethan, I—'

The moment shattered with the jarring ring of her phone. Sage glanced at the caller ID, her expression shifting into something unreadable. 'Hold that thought,' she said, before she excused herself and stepped outside to take the call.

'Right,' Ethan murmured to no one, watching her go. His heart thudded in his chest. He had only managed to utter one word, with no context around it at all, and already his insides felt as if they were being mauled by jackals. Later, he would just put an end to this misery and initiate the conversation. He would ask her to come and visit him in Queensland. Maybe some form of long-distance relationship might work, while they figured this thing out?

'Please! She's been attacked by a croc!' Ethan's hands clenched at the sound of frantic footsteps rushing into the clinic. He turned from the guinea pig he was placing back into its basket as a middle-aged man burst through the doors, his face etched with panic. He was cradling a bloodied Blue Heeler in his arms.

'Help my Belle,' the man cried again as Ethan hurried with the guinea-pig cage. Sage was close behind him and he caught the flicker of panic on her face as the man gasped with fear and exertion. The dog, a sturdy, strong animal built for the terrain of the outback, lay limp, its breathing shallow and laboured. Deep gashes marred its side and leg. Raw flesh on show made a stark contrast to the dog's dusty fur, which was matted with blood.

'Get her to surgery!' Sage barked, and Ethan led the way, the man following close behind, their footsteps echoing down the small corridor and into the next room. Ellie met them at the door, her eyes widening at the sight of the wounded creature.

'This is an emergency, cancel my next appointment,' Sage directed, her voice steady but her eyes betraying the swell of emotions he knew must be breaking inside her. Another badly injured dog. There were a lot of dogs coming in and out of here, they were the most popular pets, of course, but he'd never seen one this badly injured before.

'Easy, Belle,' he muttered, catching for the briefest second a look of such profound fear and pain in her eyes that he had to swallow back a cry of his own. Together, they transferred the dog onto the stainless-steel table. Its surface seemed extra cold and unwelcoming, even to him, as the traumatised owner stood back, wringing his hands. Gloves snapped against skin, and tools clinked as they were laid out with careful precision despite the pounding hearts in the room.

'We have multiple puncture wounds and lacerations,' Sage observed, her brow furrowing as she assessed the damage. 'We need to stop the bleeding, fast.'

Ethan helped elevate the animal. With deft fingers, he began applying gentle, steady pressure to slow the bleeding while Sage worked to clean around the wounds so they could judge the severity of the attack. The dog whined softly, her body twitching with pain despite the sedatives they had quickly administered. At least she was alive, and breathing on her own.

'Easy, Belle, you're going to be okay,' Sage murmured soothingly, working on another deep cut with a concentration that bordered on reverence. Her hands moved with an expertise honed across her years spent dedicated to healing animals. He could feel how each of her movements and whispers and treatments was a silent promise to end the suffering before her, and, as it always did, his mind went to Sage as a kid, watching the flames of the bushfire, knowing her parents and her dog were dying right in front of her.

He'd been through hell, but nothing compared to what she had… How could he inflict any more suffering on her, asking her to come to Queensland, starting something he already knew would probably end badly, one way or another? Was that the kind of life she'd want, living off-grid with him and his dad, and the horses? Without the small support network she'd gathered around her? He could move here, he supposed… but then it wouldn't be fair on Dad, Jacqueline and the kids, or his mother's legacy, which they'd vowed to honour at the homestead. The equine centre he'd established wouldn't thrive here either, not on this dry soil. His heart sank.

'Scalpel,' Sage requested, without looking up. Ethan placed it firmly in her waiting palm and watched as she carefully excised a piece of embedded tooth from the dog's hind quarters. 'Got it,' she announced, holding up the jagged remnant triumphantly before dropping it into a metal tray with a clink.

How the heck did the crocodile's tooth end up there? he wanted to ask. It must have been an old croc, or maybe a really young one? The man didn't know, he'd been so panicked at the sight of his dog in its mouth that nothing else had really registered.

'Well done, boss,' Ethan said, and her eyes softened at the genuine admiration that laced his tone. 'Let's flush these wounds and get her closed up.'

Sage reached for the saline. Together, they irrigated each and every wound meticulously once more, making sure that no trace of infection would remain and put this creature on course for any more suffering. It was a dance they knew well by now, moving around each other with a synchronicity that made him wonder sometimes if he'd ever work with another vet this well again.

What might they do if they did make something work, if she wound up moving to Queensland with him? They could open a surgery there, as his father had always planned. Dad had been pretty disappointed initially, when he'd ended up with an actress from Brisbane as a future daughter-in-law instead of a qualified veterinarian who could help mould the family business into something beyond horses. Mum's dream of a self-sufficient life, and eco-conscious activities for the community, had only just started, really. There was so much still to do, and he would do it there, with Dad, while Sage remained here, honouring her own commitments.

They continued to work seamlessly, anticipating each other's needs, passing instruments back and forth without needing to speak, and the man looked on from the corner, his face a shade of grey Ethan recognised. A special shade that seemed to be reserved for the owners of beloved animals who were fighting for their lives.

Belle's breathing steadied as they worked. As Sage finished the very last suture, a palpable sense of relief flooded the room and he removed his mask. It felt as though he hadn't drawn a breath this whole time.

'She's going to be OK,' Sage said, peeling off her gloves and giving Ethan a tired smile.

'I can't thank you both enough.' The man's voice choked as he ran his hands along the dog's head and ears, tears glistening in the corners. They told him they'd have to keep her in to monitor her, and as the man slunk off in relief and exhaustion Ethan watched Sage watching Belle. Her dedication to her work, the way she fought for each life as if it were the only one that mattered, still stirred something in his soul. It was more than professional admiration; it was a growing affection and appreciation and happiness he felt around her that he couldn't compartmentalise. It was so soon after Carrie, though, how could he trust this was even real?

'So, that was Bryce on the phone in the stable, earlier,' she said suddenly into the silence.

He turned to her, feeling the muscles in his jaw tightening. Her attention was already shifting to the paperwork that needed to be filled out.

'What does he want?' Ethan asked, guarding his tone. He should feign indifference; besides, he had nothing to be jealous of.

'He wants to visit me,' she said coolly.

'Right.'

He watched as Sage's shoulders stiffened, her body language telling him how much she hadn't wanted to divulge this information, but had decided to anyway.

'It's OK, if you really still need him to visit you,' he said. 'But what do you want from him?'

Meeting her eyes, he encouraged her silently. She was free to tell him the truth, if she wanted. She could tell him how she still deemed herself responsible for the fire that killed her parents and all the animals, and that despite everyone reminding her it wasn't her fault, including him, she was rewriting the story in her own head where she was still guilty and undeserving of forgiveness.

'Why do you still need reassurance that the bushfire wasn't your fault?' he probed. Her eyes clouded over as she looked to the side and sniffed. 'Why didn't you talk to me before you contacted Bryce?'

'I don't know what you mean.'

'Talk to me, Sage, I'm right here,' he urged. Then he realised how it sounded and backed off as her eyes narrowed. She was like Carrie right now, refusing to talk to him, or even acknowledge that she wasn't happy, despite him asking her to just be honest with him. How many months, even years, had Carrie been sleeping with Cam before he'd found out? Their communication had broken down so slowly he'd barely noticed, till she was admitting the affair.

This was supposed to be different. He'd thought, despite the challenges they faced, that what he had with Sage was a world away from anything he'd had with Carrie. But right now Sage was shutting him out on purpose, edging him off the cliff while he was blind, and he was right back where he'd started.

CHAPTER SIXTEEN

SAGE CHOPPED CARROTS with rhythmic precision, watching the sky cloud over. Each slice was pretty much a futile attempt to silence the cacophony of shrieks and laughter that were echoing through Abigail's kitchen. The kids darted around them like wild spirits, their energy the total opposite to that of the quiet, calm horses the mayor was tending to outside the window. Bad weather was coming, and already she could feel the tension in the atmosphere…although maybe some of that was of her own creation.

'Bryce called me,' Sage confessed over the din, her knife pausing mid-motion. She'd been storing up this information since that phone call and yes, OK, she was nervous. Abigail always told her things how they were, no messing. 'He wants to come to Amber Creek, to talk.'

Abigail glanced up from where she was seasoning the chicken, her brow furrowed in confusion under her fringe. 'Are you going to let him?'

'I don't know,' she said, pulling a face.

Abigail tutted. 'Why would you even consider it? Didn't he walk out on you, never to be seen again?' She made a 'poof' motion over her own head with the oregano jar.

Sage sighed, pushing a loose strand of hair behind her ear. The weight of her thoughts pressing down on her was worse than last night without Ethan in her bed. At least she'd had Belle. The Blue Heeler was good company, and it was also easier to keep a close eye on her there. She'd have been pretty much alone in the kennel in the clinic.

'Ethan's been…different since I told him. He didn't even stay over last night. He just went back to the guest house.'

'*Why* did you tell him?' Abigail said, skewering a chicken breast with a sharp look in her eyes. 'What are you doing here, Sage?'

Sage let out a long sigh as her hands faltered. Setting the knife down, she turned to face her friend, admitting she wasn't even sure. Abigail accused her of trying too hard to protect her heart, and also of thinking she didn't deserve something real, like she seemed to be building with Ethan. She said Sage was deliberately inviting in drama that would push him away. That drama, of course, being Bryce.

'You're also freaking yourself out over the chance that something will happen to Ethan and he'll leave you one way or another. Sage, these are old demons of yours—we know them well.'

'Wow.' Abigail was so wise, as well as pretty beyond measure, and successful. For a moment Sage had to laugh at how much they must have shared during all those nights they were getting to know each other, drinking wine, confessing their sins and their darkest moments. Abigail was right, of course.

'Let it go,' Abigail said, clutching her hand and pressing it to her heart. 'Let all of that go, Sage, please.'

'I know I should…'

'Please. Ethan might be guarded, but you two have something special. I've seen it. When that snake got you, I swear I saw that man's heart working overtime. Ethan is head over heels in love with you. How did you do it, by the way?'

Sage absorbed her friend's words as Abigail stirred pots and picked up shoes and reminded her kids that this wasn't a zoo and that they were not animals. Whether she was right or not about Ethan's feelings, Abigail saw through all Sage's excuses, the crazy stuff inside her own head that had been holding her captive since the fire. It was true, she sabotaged everything that threatened to bring the slightest trace of upheaval into her life, the good as well as the bad, sometimes.

'Would you move to Queensland if he asked?' Abigail's question pierced through a fresh round of screeching by the kids.

Sage held the knife suspended as the gravity

of the question sank in. 'But he hasn't asked. He did once briefly mention Queensland but then dropped it.'

'Ah.' Abigail hummed, reaching for the pepper grinder, adding a twist to the pan. 'Well, this could get awkward pretty fast. He'll be here any minute.'

Sage almost dropped the knife. 'Ethan's coming?'

'Jarrah invited him, to say thanks for everything he's done with Storm.'

Sage drew a breath that was mostly pepper. A twinge of annoyance at the mayor's impromptu decision flitted through her mind—this was supposed to be a quiet, no-stress dinner between friends—but then she couldn't blame Jarrah; Ethan had charmed him as he had everyone else. Before she could probe any further into the sudden dinner arrangement, the sound of hooves on gravel told her he was here already. Her chest tightened on the spot as she saw him through the window and Abigail gasped.

'He's riding Storm!'

Sage took a moment to process that Ethan was actually here, arriving on the back of the horse that up to this point hadn't let anyone ride him. Storm was finally healed? She wiped her hands on the apron tied around her waist, suddenly more than conscious of her flour-dusted jeans and basil-scented fingers. Not that anyone was looking at her. Ethan was the man of the moment now, Charlie and Daisy, and even the eleven-year-old Lucie were all busy cheering and whooping at his arrival.

Finally, the back door swung open. Ethan stepped inside followed by everyone else. Sage held her breath as his eyes found hers immediately.

'Hi,' she said. The intensity of his gaze magnetised her. Her feet somehow moved across the floor without her knowing. She leaned in for a kiss, her cheeks warming just attuning to his presence. It was almost instinctive now, this greeting they had shared countless times in private. She almost couldn't have helped her body's reaction to him, even standing in her best friend's kitchen, covered in flour. But as the family scattered around her, all talking at once, Ethan's hand came up gently and rested on her shoulder.

'Best not,' he said softly, so only she could hear. 'I'm still working for the mayor, remember?'

Sage stopped short. 'But Jarrah knows about us,' she protested quietly, searching his face for clarity. Was this because of what she'd said before, about inviting Bryce here?

Ethan's jaw tensed. A flicker of something unreadable passed through his eyes before he composed himself. 'It's about keeping things professional in public,' he explained, his words measured but firm.

'Right.' Sage stepped back from him, panic gripping her heart. Abigail asked her to get the plates out and help her set the table and she got to the task, head whirring. She'd helped serve a hundred meals in this house, but now she felt clumsy, opening all the wrong cupboards. He was being weird. Because of Bryce, probably. She needed to apologise, tell him how ridiculous she was being, still needing any kind of closure from her ex. Abigail was right. Bryce was just another barrier she'd erected quickly to make sure Ethan couldn't hurt her. What if they made something work, she and Ethan, something incredible, but then Ethan decided he wasn't over Carrie, and that *she* had always been a rebound? Or what if he was thrown from a horse and died... God, it was just too much for her heart to cope with, all these boomeranging emotions.

'We made chicken,' she heard herself say as she placed a plate down in front of him at the table. Her fingers knocked a fork and Ethan caught it in his lap. His eyes went to hers for a brief hot second and the look in them made her hands tremble more. Wanting him. More, now he was being so different around her. More, now that she could lose him in a hundred different ways. Storm was finally healed and he was back where he should have been weeks ago, with his family, ready to be the horse Lucie had dreamed of. Which meant Ethan would be leaving.

Sitting next to Ethan, she tried to compose herself, feeling his body heat meld with hers even though he wasn't touching her. She could be the professional veterinarian she was, the one he wanted her to be right now, but he knew her now, he knew how to tune in. He could probably tell that just by doing what he'd done, refusing a kiss, he'd made her long for him all over again...

'So, bees, huh?' Abigail started talking about the honey he'd told them about, asking Ethan all about the permaculture project and the rain-collection system he and his dad had built.

What was Ethan's father like? Sage wondered. Would she ever know? What they were trying to achieve in Queensland sounded interesting too. More than interesting, it sounded like building a sustainable future in every sense of the word. There was no possibility of anything like *here*, it was too dry and dusty for most things to thrive, whereas her practice could, in theory, be moved anywhere. OK, she would have to start again, make new friends, new relationships, new clients, but she could do that, couldn't she?

Yes. You would move to Queensland if he asked you to. You would go anywhere with him. Because you love him with your whole heart!

She watched as Ethan sliced through the tender meat, his movements deliberate and controlled. He could barely seem to look at her, except for the occasional sideways glance, like a wolf checking in on its prey. Sage's mind was drifting now, zoning out, stealing more glances at Ethan. Maybe he *was* over Carrie, but he was worried about their whirlwind romance. He just didn't want his world to be smashed to smithereens again, any more than she did.

'Ethan,' she whispered, trying to catch his hand under the table.

He pushed her away gently, but firmly.

The longer they sat there, talking about horses and bees and farmers' markets, the further away she drifted, and the more she felt him letting her. It was like a light going out between them, with Ethan operating the dimmer switch. He was tired of her already, all of these emotions that she was only half sharing. If she didn't start being totally honest with him, as his ex hadn't been, he would go and he wouldn't come back, and who would blame him?

Sage heard a toy drop to the floor above their heads. Abigail and the mayor were now upstairs, doing their best to put the kids to bed, and the warmth had all but evaporated from the room. Ethan's eyes were on her, watching her when he thought she wouldn't notice. They were alone.

'Great dinner,' he said, leaning against the doorframe across the room.

She nodded, unsure how to articulate the feeling of being on the edge of a confession that could turn her life around. He had no idea what he was doing to her, all these emotions buzzing through her, but she'd invite herself to Queensland if he didn't do it first.

'Your parents would be so proud of everything you've achieved here, Sage,' he said, his voice low. 'But, look, I didn't come here looking for anything serious.'

What?

His words hit her ears first. Everything felt hotter as the statement hit her brain, and then got at her heart, stones hurled onto glass. Ethan watched her, his expression guarded.

'What do you mean?' she stammered.

'I mean, I'm not here to start a relationship with you,' he said plainly.

His face was so dark now, and he wouldn't look at her.

'Is this because of Bryce?'

'No. Let's not forget our reality,' he said. 'This was always going to be temporary.'

The word 'temporary' echoed through her and hollowed out her belly. Temporary felt the same as worthless, as if he was off to better things already. Her heart clenched tightly, as if his actual fist had squeezed it.

'Is that truly what you want?' she asked numbly. Ethan's eyes would still not find hers. The ground felt as if it were opening up beneath her, as if everything he'd given her physically till now, the safety, the comfort, the reassurance, the love, was being retracted slowly but purposefully, as if he were pulling what was left of the snake right out of her. 'Is this because you're scared I'll run away with someone else, like Carrie did?'

'It's for the best.'

'I don't believe you.'

His face was set, his cheek turned slightly, but she stood there in silence until he was forced to look at her. Holding his gaze, she projected what she hoped was loathing and anger and disappointment, but the more he held her stare and worked his jaw, and curled his fingers to his sides, the more she knew she was only telling him she loved him. Daring him to break first. Daring him to tell her he wanted her. The more he ignored her silent confession, the harder she projected it, and the harder he rejected her.

Then he turned his head away and the slight almost sent her collapsing to the floor.

'I read you all wrong, Ethan.'

'I just wanted to make it clear, before I go,' he murmured. 'I don't want there to be any misunderstandings between us.'

Sage nodded, walking to the window and fixing her eyes on Storm, chomping on grass in the floodlit yard. There was no way in hell he was getting the satisfaction of seeing her break down and beg him to take her with him.

'Sage... I'll be leaving first thing tomorrow.'

'Go,' she said, her back still turned, where he could only see her legs shake, and not her face. Her eyes had crinkled into wet slits and her stomach was threatening to make her sick. 'Go then, Ethan. I'll tell Abigail and Jarrah you had an emergency.'

She heard his feet shuffling on the floor for a moment.

Do not turn around. Do not give him the satisfaction. Do not call out that you love him.

He left without another word. The sound of the front door closing behind him punctuated the end of their conversation, right as Abigail appeared on the stairs.

'The mayor's doing story time—' she started.

Sage slumped into a chair. Abigail rushed to her side, urging her to explain what had happened. How could those words have just come from Ethan's mouth? Abigail told her all the right things, like he was probably just freaking out and pushing her away because men were incapable of processing their emotions in a way that actually included open communication. She told her to go after him and tell him how she felt.

'I tried to, already!'

'Did you? Did you say those actual words? I love you, Ethan?'

Sage growled into her hands. He knew, he knew what she felt without her saying it. So why couldn't she just say it for real?

'You don't think you deserve him,' Abigail observed. 'But what if you're what *he* needs, Sage?'

This was ridiculous. She needed to be brave for once. Ethan had as many walls up and blind spots as she did. She'd been so focused on her own woes that she'd forgotten his. Just being around Ethan had been like opening a door she hadn't even known was there—one that had all the happy things hiding behind it. There was no guarantee that Ethan would reciprocate her feelings, or even talk to her if she followed him to the guest house and sat on his suitcase to stop him packing it. But there was no peace left in the 'what ifs' and 'maybes' any more. Things had gone well beyond that.

CHAPTER SEVENTEEN

ETHAN STOOD AT the window, his gaze fixed on the horizon as the first drops of rain on the guest-house balcony started tapping against the plants. Telling Sage he didn't want a relationship—why had he done that? Even the word relationship did not sum up what he'd imagined he'd have with her. It had been the same story the entire time he'd been here, knowing he wanted her, but knowing what had happened the last time he'd felt like this. Going through that again could hollow a man out.

He glanced at the caller ID on his buzzing phone. Jacqueline. 'Hey, sis.'

'Ethan—did you book your return flight yet? The kids are asking when you're coming to finish that game of Jenga with them. You know, they haven't touched it since you left.'

His tone was nonchalant, bordering on dismissive as he told her about the flight delays and the storm, but she saw right through it. 'OK, what's wrong?'

There was a softness to Jacqueline's prompt that loosened his tongue. He explained what he could, how he'd blown something small out of proportion in his head. She asked if he was feeling overwhelmed because it was happening so soon after Carrie, and he stopped himself saying, *Yes, everything is because of Carrie,* because what was the point? He said nothing and Jaqueline, who knew him, told him he wasn't giving things a fair chance, because Carrie was not Sage.

He bristled at the comparison, unsure how to articulate the fear of being vulnerable again that had rooted itself so deeply in his bones. Instead he paced the wooden floorboards and kicked at a fallen coat hanger.

'It was just a bit of fun, you know, and I took it too far, and now… I have to forget about her.'

'Ethan. Why don't you just give her a chance?'

'I don't want to give her a chance.'

Jacqueline sighed deeply and he almost felt her eyes roll. 'Well, you're an idiot, even though I love you. Sounds like you love *her,* too. Just remember the love, brother, and you'll be fine. I gotta go.'

Ethan clenched his fist as she hung up, the phone still tight against his ear. His breath hitched. 'It's not love,' he muttered into the emptiness, as if he could possibly convince the walls— or himself at this point. 'I do *not* love Sage.'

The words fell flat. The lie felt like a physical ache in his chest as he paced the cramped space between the bed and the window. 'Sage doesn't need someone like me. She's better off alone.' Even as he said it out loud, he was picturing her laughter, all the times she'd caught him kicking the old coffee machine. When Sage forgot herself and the pain and guilt she wore like a badge of honour, she had the kind of laugh that stopped time. *All you want to do when you hear a laugh like that,* he thought, *is keep it going, and lose your own dark thoughts in the light.*

As long as he lived he would never stop seeing the way she'd looked just now when he'd hurt her with his words. She'd looked as if she'd never laugh again, as if he'd stolen something new and precious and irreplaceable, something maybe he'd gone some way to providing, right out from under her. And he loved her even more after he'd done it, because no one had ever looked at him with that much love, especially when he was taking it away.

All the times he'd told himself he didn't want a relationship bucked at his insides; it wasn't true, not when it was Sage. It was just…impossible… to know for certain that she wouldn't come to his home and be with him, and his father, and his horses, and promise him for ever, and make him want to have her babies, and then do the same thing Carrie had done. Not that she would do that—she wasn't Carrie—but how could he really be sure something else wouldn't go wrong, and take him right back to square one? He just had to trust that she wouldn't. He *could* trust her not to hurt him, he realised. But now he'd gone all out to ruin what they had on purpose. If she never forgave him, he wouldn't be surprised.

He tried to call her. It rang off. Of course, why would she pick up the phone to him now? She was probably fuming. He knew she didn't really want Bryce here. And instead of sympathising with her attempts to protect herself, and giving her the reassurance that she still needed, or fighting for *them* and telling her to forget Bryce and come and see his home in Queensland instead, where she could make love to him in the study, and the cabin and the greenhouse, meet his horses, meet his sister…instead of doing any of that, he'd shut her down.

Dialling her again, he bit his nails and waited. And waited.

She's clicked off again!

'Tomorrow,' he growled, eyeing the fierce storm. The word felt like less of a promise to himself and more like a lifeline right now, some remaining tiny tether to the kind of life he could have with her if he'd just get out of his own damn head and reach for it.

Tomorrow he would find Sage and mend what

he'd smashed to pieces—or, at the very least, try and explain to her why he'd felt the need to break it in the first place.

Sage was seething. She'd been seething when she'd gone to sleep after getting back home in the rain, and now, waking up after only an hour to the ominous skies overhead, she was even angrier.

How dare he humiliate me like that? But I still love him.

'Come here, girl,' she said to Belle, putting a plate of kibble down close to the Blue Heeler on the bed, so she wouldn't have to walk for it on her bad leg. Realistically it probably wasn't right to have the dog on the bed, but she'd been such good company last night after what she'd overheard from the other side of that guest-house door.

'It was just a bit of fun, you know, and I took it too far, and now I just have to forget about her... I don't want to give her a chance.'

Sage pressed her face into the pillow. It smelled of him, his scent, the animal and the gentle lover, taking turns to savour and worship her, giving her space and time to explore him in return. She'd seen inside him. Let him inside her.

How could I have been so stupid over this man, so many times?

'I went there to make things right,' she said, tossing the pillow to the floor. Belle swiped her hand with her hot tongue in understanding. 'I mean, I actually thought I would hear him say he wanted me to at least go with him to Queensland. I thought he was going to say we should try. As if men just change like that!'

Thinking back to the tone of his voice through the door, it had struck her more than his words. He'd made it very clear that whatever had been between them, it wasn't what she'd thought. '*I do* not *love Sage*,' he'd said, definitively.

To think how determined she'd been, marching to the guest house earlier this evening...then realising she didn't know his room number. And she didn't have a key. And she'd left her phone at Abigail's. It was still there, probably tucked down the sofa on silent mode. She'd set it that way in case Bryce called back; she would have to let him know she didn't want him to visit any more, but it was too much to deal with now. What a mess.

After Babs had let her into the guest house and pointed to Ethan's room, which weirdly she had never been to this whole time, she'd raised her hand to his door and prepared herself to show him exactly why it would be a crime not to see if this connection could be something worth salvaging...and expanding...for a little bit longer. Or for ever. This kind of emotional roller coaster was a sign that the path was right for both of them, but obviously the way there was always going to be rocky, considering the challenges that faced them.

But then, Ethan had been on the phone, probably to his father or sister. Oh…what an idiot she'd made of herself going over there. He was probably at the airport now, counting down the minutes till they started rescheduling the flights. Her heart burned till the anger turned to tears that threatened to soak poor Belle's head.

A crash of thunder. Sage sat up and blinked in shock. Great, a storm was definitely on its way. 'Stay here,' she ordered Belle. 'I have to go check on the other animals.'

The isolation pressed in on her as she checked on the few animal patients they had—a tortoise, a cat and a wallaby. It wasn't unusual for her to be alone in the clinic, her patients often kept her at work long after the others had gone, but now, on top of everything with Ethan, the solitude felt a lot like abandonment. The air was thick with electricity, too, a tangible intensity that put her even more on edge.

Another crash, closer this time, sent a jolt of dread to her bones. It sounded too close for comfort. She whipped around, her eyes landing on the window. The sight rooted her to the spot.

No, no, no, not again!

A bolt of lightning must have struck her cabin. Smoke was curling out from somewhere she couldn't see. Fear knotted in her stomach. Not again, she couldn't face this again!

Then… 'Belle! Belle is in there.'

Somehow, Sage forced herself to the phone and called in the emergency. They'd take too long to get here, though. The flames were erupting from the roof now, greedily devouring shingles and wood with an insatiable hunger as her legs propelled her outside. The cabin was fully ablaze and poor Belle was still trapped inside. The world seemed to pitch and toss as Sage took a step forward on trembling legs.

'Belle!' she called out, as if the dog might appear through the closed door. The flames before her eyes were dancing with an eerie familiarity. She was back to that night again, when the same orange tongues of fire had greedily licked at the tents and trees and sky and robbed her of everything she'd known and loved. The sheer magnitude of what she was about to do settled in her chest like lead. The same terror rendered her immobile as a frightened child, clawing at her insides and threatening to paralyse her again.

But... Belle. The thought of the poor dog, trapped and afraid, spurred her forward. She wasn't a child any more. And she could finally see, through adult eyes, that what had happened back then had never been her fault. She had let the guilt and fear eat her up, and now she'd lost the love of her life to Queensland. But there was no way she was letting Belle die today. Belle needed her.

Sage dashed towards the cabin, the heat radiating off the structure, pushing back against her advance. Miraculously the front door was still clear; the lightning must have struck at the back.

Come on, Sage, you can do this.

The door was a barrier of heat, but she forced it open with both hands. Smoke billowed out to greet her and met with the dust in the wind. Her vision impaired, she coughed, her eyes stinging as she searched for the bedroom door through the haze. The glow of the fire crept under the door to the kitchen and painted monstrous shadows on the walls like a gallery of all her worst fears coming to life.

You can do this.

'Belle!' Her voice was a desperate plea, hoarse and cracking. Smoke cloaked her as she staggered over the threshold, her lungs screaming for clean air. She could barely see a thing, but she wasn't backing away this time. She would not let history repeat itself. There was no way the fire was taking anything else from her, not if she could help it.

But before she could move any further, a firm hand clasped around her arm, wrenching her back. Ethan stood there on the porch, solid and unyielding, his deep blue eyes boring into hers with an intensity that matched the heat. His ute was behind him, the engine still running.

'Sage, what are you doing?'

She shook her head, wild and frantic. What was

he doing here? 'Belle is in the bedroom, Ethan! I have to—'

His expression shifted as he coughed, something like understanding softening the hard lines of his face. 'Stay here,' he ordered her. Without another word, he released her and sprinted past her, the muscles in his back flexing beneath his shirt as he propelled himself towards the bedroom.

'Ethan!' she screamed after him.

Her heart lurched into her throat as she watched him disappear into the smoke. She screamed his name again, but it turned into a cough. Reluctantly she stood back. Sirens wailed somewhere in the distance and her hands clenched into fists at her sides. The possibility of losing him strangled her with every second that ticked by with her pulse hammering in her ears.

Why had he come back here anyway, after everything he'd said to whoever it was on the phone? Unless she'd missed a piece of the puzzle somehow. She'd been rattled and upset; she could have been creating another narrative, as she'd probably done about Bryce! That fortress Ethan had built around his emotions—he'd just smashed that completely to pieces by coming back here despite the fierce storm, obviously to see her. And now he'd dived into the blaze for her, for Belle.

'Ethan!' Her voice was a raw, guttural cry as she sank back into the depths of terror. The clinic behind her felt like another world, safe and sterile, while she stood here, heart thundering against her ribs, literally on the precipice of her worst nightmare. He had gone after Belle, for her, without a second thought. What if he didn't come out? His selflessness was a blade to her heart suddenly—what if she lost him, too?

The sirens grew louder. She imagined him struggling against the smoke and heat in there and desperately tried to hold onto her belief in his strength and resourcefulness. He was the strongest person she knew! But doubt crept in just as fast, whispering that maybe she was wrong. Maybe he wasn't strong enough. Fire took everything away and she knew it. Seconds felt like hours. Her mind conjured images of him overcome by smoke, succumbing to the heat, and she shook her head fiercely, trying to dispel the thoughts. No, he *was* strong, he could do this.

'Please, Ethan,' she whispered, her voice breaking. 'Please.'

How long had he been gone? Thirty seconds? It felt like a lifetime. The heat pushed against her as if warning her back, but she took a step forward, then another, her body moving with a will of its own. She couldn't let fear paralyse her again, not when it mattered most. She was about to go in after him, when a silhouette forged through the smoke. 'Ethan!'

He was grey from the ashes, arms cradling the limp Belle. 'Get back!' he commanded, his voice rough with smoke but edged with an iron-clad resolve as he urged her away from the door, back to the forecourt. Sage turned to see firefighters jumping out of their truck, unravelling hoses and yelling commands to each other as their battle with the blaze consuming her home began. The urgency of the scene, and the fact that her home and everything in it were being destroyed, barely registered with Sage; all that mattered in that moment was the man in front of her now, leading her through the doors to the smoke-free clinic. The phone was ringing off the hook.

Belle squirmed in Ethan's grip, coming to life as the fresh air filled her lungs. The relief was overpowering as he laid the dog down carefully. With the chaos unfolding outside, Sage reached up and pulled him into a kiss that she hoped held all the words she'd left unspoken, and could barely have uttered if she'd tried.

'Ethan,' she choked out eventually, hands in his ash-filled hair, her voice croaky from smoke. 'I would never have survived losing you! What are you doing here?'

Ethan's expression softened as he put one large hand to the back of her neck and drew her against him. 'You were about to run into the fire,' he said in awe, stroking her cheek with his thumb. 'You! Sage, do you realise what could have happened to you?'

'I couldn't let Belle die.'

'And you would have done the same thing for your parents, if you could have. If you hadn't been a terrified child back then. Do you see that now?'

She closed her eyes, pressed her forehead to his. 'I know, I do know that.'

'I was talking to my sister about you,' he admitted, his voice carrying over the tumultuous sounds of gushing water and men shouting, and the phone still ringing off the hook. 'She kindly reminded me I was in denial...but I love you, Sage. I do. I've fallen in love with you.'

Sage's heart hammered against her chest as he kissed her again, and Belle sat up, confused but perfectly fine apparently.

'I overheard you talking,' she said, her lips still an inch from his. 'In the guest house... I came to talk to you after you left Abigail's. I thought—'

'You thought what?' Ethan's brow furrowed, his concern palpable.

'I thought you said you *didn't* love me. That we were just having fun or something.' A bitter laugh escaped her lips, and she shook her head. 'But I only caught part of it, didn't I?'

Ethan cupped her face, his thumbs gently wiping away the ash that must have been coating her cheeks as much as his. 'You heard the fear talking, Sage. My fear of admitting what I really feel for you. But I want you to always talk to me, always tell me everything, OK? We can work anything out, as long as we talk about it.'

She saw it then—the way his eyes shimmered with intensity, the way his hands trembled ever so slightly as they held her. It was raw vulnerability, and it struck at the very core of her being. She hadn't been honest about why she'd really considered asking Bryce here—as if she needed to hear anything from him at all when she had Ethan right here, painting a picture of the truth, plain and simple.

'I've been pushing you away, Ethan, I have, because I was scared,' she confessed, 'of losing someone I love all over again. And you—'

'Guilty as charged,' he said softly, tipping her chin up to meet his gaze. 'I think you should come to Queensland. What do you think?'

Sage felt a shift inside her that felt like chains falling off. She could hardly help her smile as his hands found hers. 'I hope you're not just saying that because my house just burnt down,' she teased.

'I'm saying it because I've fallen madly in love with you,' he replied, a grin tugging at the corner of his mouth. 'How many more times do you want me to say it?'

'As many times as you like, don't ever stop,'

she said, kissing him again. In that moment she knew she would go anywhere with him, and for him. Everything was going to be just fine.

EPILOGUE

SAGE PERCHED ON the edge of the veranda, her feet barely grazing the sun-warmed wood beneath them. She took a slow sip of the honey lemonade they had made together yesterday with Kara and Jayson, and some of the other kids from the local school, loving how the sweetness of it danced on her tongue. Ethan sat beside her, his gaze scanning the horizon where the new horse with the limp would soon appear.

'When does it get here?' Sage asked, breaking the comfortable silence that had settled between them as he sat at the long wooden table, addressing a file of paperwork.

'Soon. I'll have my work cut out with this one, but we'll get there,' he replied, his tone reflecting the calm certainty that always surrounded him when it came to his equine patients here at the homestead.

'You always do,' she told him. There was always a steady stream of horses coming in and out and most days Ethan spent his time outside with them. Occasionally he would fill in at the small clinic they'd just opened on the property, but that was her project really. Setting up a whole new practice in Queensland hadn't been too complicated in the end. Of course, she missed her regular patients, but Ellie and Billy had a new chief vet now, with the fees coming out of Amber Creek's budget, and the community was thriving even without her. And now she had a growing rota of even more regulars and wonderful connections, with both the local animals and people. She had also joined a book club and a swimming club in an effort to socialise outside work; something she hadn't dreamed of doing before, when she'd been too busy judging herself in her own head to make many friends.

The dogs, a ragtag crew of rescue mutts, were sprawled out in contentment around their feet. Their tails thumped in lazy acknowledgment any time one of them was addressed. Their presence was a comforting constant to Sage these days, a reminder of the simple pleasures that life on their little homestead had brought her since the move, although, as hard as they tried, they would never add as much comedy value as Joey.

Sage glanced over to the paddock, where their rescue kangaroo was engaged in his own brand of morning exercise. With each buoyant leap, Joey seemed to defy the very notion of gravity, and a chuckle escaped Sage as she watched him dart after a bird. It was impossible not to find him funny; the kids all loved him.

'You know, he can hop off anywhere, whenever he wants,' Ethan said, catching her eye with a shared sense of amusement. 'But he chooses to hang out around here. Because you rescued him as a baby. You're his mother now.'

'I hope he never leaves,' she told him, her laughter fading into a softer smile. Her hand drifted instinctively to her stomach, resting gently on the curve that had only just begun to show. Three months along, and already the life within her stirred a protective love she hadn't known she possessed.

Ethan stood, and in seconds his big hand was covering hers, the strength in his fingers a reassurance. 'How are you feeling? Any more morning sickness?'

'Better today,' she admitted, more than grateful for his unwavering support in what would have been a somewhat jarring experience without him, feeling her body grow and change day by day. His fierce protectiveness had been a surprise at first, especially when he'd refused to let her ride anywhere alone, but now she knew it was all born from his love for her.

'Remember, no overdoing it,' he said, his thumb brushing across her skin in a tender caress. 'That includes worrying about our new arrival.'

Sage smiled. 'Promise,' she whispered, watching a bee hover over the plants she'd just potted along the edge of the veranda. The new irrigation system was a success, and they'd even given a workshop the other day in town, teaching others how to harvest greywater and rainwater, as she and Ethan had done in Amber Creek before bringing the new skills here with them. Sometimes she thought about that place, how it had all been rebuilt after the fire. Only her record player had been salvaged. Abigail and the mayor had brought it over when they'd come to visit, and she kept it here now, in what was going to be the baby's nursery.

She inhaled the scent of eucalyptus from the surrounding trees, letting it steady her nerves. Ethan looked up, his deep blue eyes reflecting a curiosity that told her how attuned to her he was. 'What's going on?' he asked.

'I've been thinking,' she began, 'about names for the baby.'

'Have you, now?' His lips curved into an expectant smile, lemonade forgotten.

'Actually, I already have one in mind.' She watched his face, seeking assurance, needing to know if he agreed with her. 'I was thinking… about naming him after my father if it's a boy. Or my mum if it's a girl.'

Ethan's reaction was immediate, his happiness sending butterflies swooping through her. 'Anthony or Caroline. I love that. Your parents would be honoured,' he said, and the excitement in his tone gave way to a warmth that wrapped around her heart.

'Really?' The doubt in her voice was a whisper of her old fears, but she let it wash away as he dashed his hands through his hair, grinning before kissing her and lifting her from her feet.

'Absolutely,' he affirmed, pulling back just enough to meet her gaze again. 'It's perfect.'

The creak of the veranda gate made them both look up. Ethan's father, John, emerged from his part of the homestead, a basket of eggs in one hand. He offered a knowing grin as he caught the tail end of their intimate exchange.

'Morning, you two,' he called out, approaching with a stride as familiar as Ethan's. 'Fresh eggs for breakfast.'

'Thanks, Dad.' Ethan shifted his stuff to make room for his father at the table.

Sage studied John's face. It was etched with the wisdom of years and the kindness that he always seemed to bestow on her when she needed it most. Living with Ethan's father on the property was great. Not only did the two of them seem to have endless topics to discuss whenever it was just them, but he'd brought an unexpected kind of solace too. While her adopted father and mother had visited several times already and always made the place feel more like home, in a way, John was filling a void left by her own biological dad's absence. It wasn't the same, of course—nothing could be—but it was a comfort that further dulled the edges of her loss, and she knew without a doubt her own parents would have loved him too. They would have loved this whole place.

'Any special plans for today?' John asked. The twinkle in his eye suggested he knew more than he let on.

'Just taking it easy,' Sage replied, sharing a glance with Ethan. Sometimes she wondered if they'd ever been caught making love; it was impossible to always keep quiet, and John had a habit of pottering about the place on his chores in the yard. Luckily he was pretty relaxed about that sort of thing. Ethan had said before now that his dad was different now, less shrouded in grief, and more like he used to be. He insisted they had Sage to thank for bringing a new lease of life to the property, but Sage knew Ethan was probably different too. They were both a work in progress, but somehow they made things work. Communication was everything. And their love.

'I was thinking I might make some calls today, tell people about the baby,' she said.

'Good, good.' John nodded. He glanced at Ethan, his voice softening. 'You know, I'm so proud of the family you're starting, son. It's going to be good for you, for all of us.'

Sage's heart swelled. Ethan reached under the

table and gave her hand a squeeze. 'Let's call Abigail first,' Ethan suggested. His blue eyes sparkled with the kind of anticipation that made Sage's heart do a somersault. The news they were about to share was big, life-changing and, oh, so gossip-worthy. Abigail was going to flip out, not least because this had happened so soon after the wedding.

Sage had only just come off birth control when the faint blue line on the pregnancy test had had her weeping with both joy and fear in the toilet cubicle of a Brisbane shopping centre. Fear because she hadn't the faintest idea how to be a parent. Ethan had soon taken that fear away though. He always liked to say that they could handle anything together, and she knew just by looking around this place that he was right.

Sage watched him dial, her fingers absently tracing the rim of her lemonade glass. 'Abigail? It's Ethan. Could you put me on speaker? Sage has something to tell you.'

The line crackled slightly before Abigail's familiar voice filled the air, bubbling with warmth. 'Hey, you two! To what do I owe the pleasure?'

'Hi,' Sage chimed in, her pulse quickening. She took a deep breath, feeling Ethan's supportive gaze upon her. 'We wanted to tell you first... I'm pregnant.'

There was a moment of stunned silence before Abigail erupted into squeals that could have woken the entire countryside. 'No way! Are you serious? Oh, my goodness, congratulations!'

Sage laughed, relief flooding through her. Sharing this secret with her best friend had just lifted a weight she hadn't realised she'd been carrying. 'We're over the moon,' she confessed.

'I wish I could hug you right now!' Abigail cried, and the longing in her voice travelled across the miles, making Sage blink back a sudden tear.

'Us too,' Ethan agreed, his strong hand finding Sage's again.

'Remember the wedding, Sage? When the kids chased the chickens around the coop and collected eggs like they were treasure? They'll have a little cousin to teach them all the farm tricks too, soon,' Abigail mused aloud, sending Sage's mind drifting back to that day five months ago.

'It was a great day.'

'It was magical,' Abigail agreed as they reminisced. 'They've been asking to help sort the recycling and throw coffee on the compost heap ever since. I don't know how you did it. They want to visit you again soon.'

'They're always welcome.' Sage smiled, picturing her friend's children's faces all lit up with wonder...dirt smudged on their cheeks despite their best smart outfits for the wedding.

'Speaking of warm welcomes, we should let you go. We've got a new horse coming in today that needs some love and care,' Ethan interjected, mindful as always of their responsibilities.

'Of course, you busy bees,' Abigail said playfully. 'Take care of yourselves, and that little miracle too. Love you both.'

'Love you too,' they echoed before hanging up.

Sage leaned back in her chair, the lightness in her chest spreading through her entire being. She glanced at Ethan, who was already lost in his thoughts, watching the gates for the horse. She could barely believe she'd got so lucky. How had it happened to her? Soon they'd be nurturing more than just animals here; they'd be raising a child of their own.

'Are you going to be OK here for a while, Mrs Matthews?' Ethan asked as the horse and its owner appeared ahead. He reached across to tenderly brush a strand of hair from her face, then bent to drop a kiss to her belly.

'Always, Mr Matthews,' she replied, her eyes locking with his. Sage knew without a trace of doubt that she was home, and safe, and for as long as he was with her, she always would be.

* * * * *